Anonymous

Guide through Mount Auburn: a hand-book for passengers over the Cambridge railroad

Illustrated with engravings and a plan of the cemetery. Sixth Edition

Anonymous

Guide through Mount Auburn: a hand-book for passengers over the Cambridge railroad
Illustrated with engravings and a plan of the cemetery. Sixth Edition

ISBN/EAN: 9783337208592

Printed in Europe, USA, Canada, Australia, Japan

Cover: Foto ©Lupo / pixelio.de

More available books at **www.hansebooks.com**

GUIDE THROUGH MOUNT AUBURN.

A

HAND-BOOK

FOR

Passengers over the Cambridge Railroad.

ILLUSTRATED WITH ENGRAVINGS

AND

A PLAN OF THE CEMETERY.

SIXTH EDITION.

BOSTON:
PUBLISHED BY BRICHER & RUSSELL,
129 WASHINGTON STREET.
1865.

CONTENTS.

Entered, according to Act of Congress, in the year 1859, by
BRICHER & RUSSELL,
In the Clerk's Office of the District Court of the District of Massachusetts.

INTRODUCTORY.

CAMBRIDGE is principally noted throughout the country as the seat of the oldest College in the United States. The town, originally called *Newtowne*, was settled in 1630, soon after the settlement of Boston. It had originally a very large extent of territory, the greater portion of which has since been set off, and now forms several of the adjoining towns. "Scarcely had the venerable founders of New England felled the trees of the forest," says Dr. Holmes, in his American Annals, "when they began to provide means to insure the stability of their colony. Learning and religion they wisely judged to be the firmest pillars of the commonwealth." In 1636, the General Court appropriated four hundred pounds towards the erection of a public school at Newtowne. In 1638, John Harvard, a minister of Charlestown, left by will nearly eight hundred pounds, to be devoted to the support of this school. The General Court soon after ordered that the school, in honor of its earliest benefactor, should be called Harvard College, and the town Cambridge, in memory of the place in England at whose university several of the most influential of the colonists had received their education. From that day to this, the College has been carried on successfully, constantly increasing in reputation throughout the country and the world, until now it is the best endowed of all our colleges, and with regard to library, professorships, and other literary advantages in general, it is the first institution of its kind in the United States. Hayward, in his Massachusetts Gazetteer, says truly that "the establishment of this College, 'consecrated to Christ and the Church,' has been generally regarded as a striking proof of the far-seeing wisdom of the fathers of Massachusetts. It shared the prayers and best wishes of ministers and churches, and proved the nursery of many 'plants of renown,' distinguished, not in the walks of sacred labor alone, but in council, at the bar, upon the bench, and even in the field." Several of the most talented men of New England have been proud of the

(3)

title of President of Harvard College, and hosts of others, whose names are borne upon the college rolls of graduates, have, in years past, adorned, and still continue to adorn, the social, religious, political, and professional circles of every portion of the country.

In later years, Cambridge has become noted as containing the entrance to the beautiful Cemetery at Mount Auburn, which is situated partly in Cambridge, and partly in the adjoining town of Watertown.

It may be imagined that the location of a College at Cambridge rendered necessary, in early times, the contrivance of some means for public conveyance between the town on one side of Charles River, near its mouth, and what was then, and for many years after, the metropolis of the country, — Boston, — on a peninsula, on the opposite side of the mouth of the river. The only possible means of communication between the two places *by land*, was by passage over Boston Neck, through Roxbury, a long and tedious journey when compared with the short distance between the two towns by water. The ordinary method of public conveyance was therefore, in those early days, by means of a small ferry boat, which plied between the two places.

The two towns had no other means of direct communication between them until the erection of what is known as the West Boston Bridge, which was built across Charles River, and finished in the year 1793. This bridge was one of the first structures of the kind in the country. It is the one over which the Cambridge Railroad passes, and will be referred to more at length hereafter. The construction of this bridge added much to the importance of Cambridge, and its population has, as an evidence thereof, been rapidly increasing ever since its erection. In the year 1846, the town received a municipal charter from the state legislature, and assumed the form of city government common in New England, essentially the same as that of Boston. The place now, in 1858, has a population of about twenty-five thousand inhabitants. Should it increase in population as rapidly as it has for some few years past, it will before many years be one of the most populous of New England cities.

Cambridge is naturally divided into four parts : *Old Cambridge*, which contains the Colleges and Mount Auburn Cemetery ; *North Cambridge*, beyond the College, in a northerly direction, toward the town of West Cambridge ; *Cambridgeport*, which embraces the territory between the end of

West Boston Bridge and Old Cambridge; and *East Cambridge*, the most recently settled part of the city, which is reached from Boston by another bridge, called Canal or Craigie's Bridge, a short distance north of the West Boston Bridge. East Cambridge, to a much greater extent than any of the other parts of the city, is devoted to manufacturing purposes. The works of the New England and Bay State Glass Companies are in this part of the city, where large numbers of persons find employment. There is considerable manufacturing carried on at Cambridgeport, and Old Cambridge has acquired some notoriety from the fact that within its boundaries are located several of the largest printing offices and stereotype founderies in the country. It is here that the plates of a large portion of the *standard* works published in Boston are cast, and it is here that the works themselves are printed. The first printing press in America was established in Cambridge, in 1639, by Stephen Day, and the first work printed thereon was "The Freeman's Oath." North Cambridge is principally noted for its cattle fairs, where immense numbers of cattle are sold weekly.

Although, as has been remarked, Cambridge is to a certain extent a manufacturing place, much more so than the generality of suburban towns, yet, as will readily be imagined from a knowledge of its proximity to the capital, and the ready means of public conveyance between the two places, it is, and always must be, a place occupied principally for residences of persons doing business in the metropolis. The construction of the Horse Railroad has to an unusual extent contributed to make Cambridge desirable as a place of residence; and when it is remembered that the centre of the city is within half an hour's ride of the business part of Boston, that the city is supplied with gas, and furnished with a most abundant supply of the purest water, it would seem that a residence there must be almost as convenient as a residence in Boston, besides having all those attractions so eagerly *wished for* in a large city, and always *expected* in a country residence.

PUBLIC CONVEYANCES.

It may be interesting now to glance at the various means of public conveyance between the two cities, from the earli-

1 *

est times to the present day. The old ferry boat has already been noticed, as having been the only direct method of conveyance between the two places, from the settlement of Cambridge until the year 1793. Let the reader imagine, if he can, the appearance of the affair, which, in all probability, was nothing but a small row boat; then imagine the building of the new bridge, and what a wonder it must have been to the inhabitants, who saw, as it were, their town of Cambridge joined arm in arm with the metropolis; then imagine the first coach that was used to convey passengers from Old Cambridge to Boston, then the long omnibuses, and finally the horse cars.

THE OMNIBUSES.

For nearly two years after the ferry was abolished, and the bridge completed, there were no means by which the people of Cambridge and Boston could visit each other, except by a long walk from place to place over the bridge, or by the use of private conveyances. In 1795, Nathaniel Stimson and Joseph Seaver commenced running a coach to Boston twice a day. The coach was an ancient affair, was drawn by two horses, and carried eight persons, besides the driver. The driver in those days announced his approach with sound of a horn. In 1797, the originators of the enterprise sold out their interest to Jonathan Hersey, who ran the coaches until 1805 or 1806. Mr. Hersey then sold out to James Read. Mr. Read afterwards sold out to a Mr. Fuller, but subsequently bought back again, and continued to run the coach until 1828. In 1826, Ebenezer Kimball commenced running a *hired* hack from Cambridgeport every *other* hour. This enterprise was so successful, that he purchased a second-hand coach, and put it upon the route. In 1828, he purchased Mr. Read's interest in the Old Cambridge coach. Near this time, the use of the horn was discontinued, and a bugle substituted. The coaches were then drawn by four horses. The first *omnibus* was placed on the route on Commencement Day, 1834. In 1837, another omnibus was placed by Mr. Kimball on the route, and was run every other half hour. This was soon followed by another omnibus.

In 1839, what was long known as the Cambridge Stage Company was formed, composed of Abel Willard, Mark Bills, and Charles Haynes, who purchased all Mr. Kimball's interest, and continued to run two hourly and two half hourly coaches from Old Cambridge. Occasional coaches, running on Harvard Street and Broadway, were commenced in 1843. In November, 1843, Mr. Tarbox started an opposition coach, and in January, 1844, a regular opposition line was started by Messrs. Tarbox and Stearns. Mr. Stearns afterwards became sole proprietor of the opposition, united with the regular line, and commenced running every quarter of an hour. In 1847, two coaches were placed on Harvard Street, and a rival line on Broadway was purchased. Messrs. Willard and Stearns afterwards admitted Charles A. Kimball, son of Ebenezer Kimball, as a partner in the concern, and from that time until the establishment of the railroad, the business was carried on by Messrs. Willard, Stearns, and Kimball, running trips every quarter of an hour, and oftener, when required. As soon as the railroad was completed, they made an amicable arrangement with the Union Railway Company, to whom the railroad had been leased, by which all their omnibuses, sleighs, horses, harnesses, &c., were passed over to the new company.

THE HORSE RAILROAD.

In the year 1853, several public spirited gentlemen applied to the legislature for a charter, with power to build a horse railroad from Boston to Roxbury. An application was made soon after by several gentlemen of Cambridge for a charter with like power to construct a horse railroad from Boston to Cambridge. In May, 1853, a charter was granted to the Roxbury company, and, a few days afterwards, another charter was granted to Gardiner G. Hubbard, Isaac Livermore, Charles C. Little, their associates and successors, under the name of the Cambridge Railroad Company. Nothing was done, however, under the charter, except locating the road, until the year 1855, when a contract was made with Gardner Warren for the construction of the road. Work under this contract was commenced September 1, 1855, and the road was so far completed on the 26th of March, 1856, that cars were run upon it on that day for the first time. The road had previously been leased to the Union Railway Company, another corporation, who purchased of the old omnibus proprietors all their interest and good will on the 1st of January, 1856, at which time they commenced running the omnibuses until the cars could be put upon the track. The omnibuses soon afterwards disappeared altogether.

The Cambridge road was the *first* horse railroad actually in operation in New England, although the Roxbury company was chartered a few days before the Cambridge company.

The road extends in a direct line to the College buildings, thence to Mount Auburn, and runs thence to Watertown Village. There are also branch tracks; one from the College buildings, through North Cambridge to the West Cambridge line, where a connection is made with the West Cambridge Railroad, which runs thence to the centre of West Cambridge; another branch from Cambridgeport to East Cambridge, and another from Cambridgeport through River Street to the Brighton line, where a connection is made with the Newton Railroad, which runs thence through Brighton. A line from East Cambridge to the College buildings, through Cambridge street, is projected, and will probably be completed before the issue of this work. The distances on these roads are

From Boston to Mount Auburn Stables, . .	5 miles.
" Mount Auburn to Watertown, . . .	2 "
	7 miles.
Length of North Cambridge branch, . . .	2¼ "
" " River street branch, ...	¾ "
" " East Cambridge branch, . . .	¾ "
" " Cambridge street branch, . . .	2 "
Total length of road operated by the Union Railway Company, ...	12¾ miles.

The length of the connecting roads not operated by the Union Railway Company are as follows : —

West Cambridge Railroad, . . .	about 3 miles.
Newton Railroad, ...	3 "
	6 miles.

Making a total of nearly 19 miles of connected Horse Railroad.

The equipment used by the Union Railway Company, consists of about 50 cars, 300 horses and other necessary articles, buildings, &c. The cars run about 275 trips per day, a trip being the journey from one terminus to another and back again. The average number of passengers carried over the road in a day is about 8000. The company employs regularly about 140 persons. The Union Railway Company have been remarkably successful since the opening of the road, and have not only paid their rent, their running expenses, and kept the road in repair, but have also paid to their own stockholders ten per cent. per annum.

THE ROUTE.

[The visitor is supposed to be going toward Cambridge.]

Supposing the visitor to be now seated in one of the cars from Boston, that the bell has been rung, and the car started, we will endeavor to accompany him, and point out objects of interest as they are passed.

DR. LOWELL'S CHURCH.

The street leading from the car station in Bowdoin Square, Boston, to the West Boston Bridge, before referred to, is called Cambridge Street. Just as the car begins to descend the hill, a large open space will be noticed on the right hand side of the street, with a small fountain in its centre. This square is called Lowell Square, and the church beyond, the West Church. Here the Rev. Dr. Lowell formerly preached. The society was formed in 1735, and the present church was erected in 1806, at about which time Dr. Lowell was settled as pastor. In 1837, Rev. Cyrus A. Bartol became colleague with Dr. Lowell, since which time Dr. Lowell has not attended to the active duties of his office.

THE MEDICAL COLLEGE.

At a short distance from the bridge is a small street called North Grove Street, leading from the right hand side of the street, at the end of which may be seen a large brick building, called the Massachusetts Medical College. This institution is properly a branch of Harvard College, the medical students attending here to hear lectures from the various professors. The building will accommodate several hundred students, has a large anatomical museum, and a well-selected medical library. The proximity of the College to the Massachusetts General Hospital affords students a fine opportunity to witness a great variety of interesting cases. By his will, Dr. John C. Warren ordered that his skeleton, properly prepared, should be presented to the institution, the objects of which he materially promoted during his lifetime. The Medical College is interesting as being the scene of the murder of Dr. George Parkman by Dr. John W. Webster, on the 23d of November, 1849. Dr. Parkman was a gentleman of wealth residing in Boston, who had loaned to Dr. Webster, the professor of chemistry at Harvard College, a sum of money, which he had made repeated attempts to obtain. On the day named above, he called at Dr. Webster's office in the Medical College, and demanded the money. It was refused, and high words passed between the two, when Dr. Webster struck Dr. Parkman with a stick near at hand, and killed him. Dr. Webster then attempted to destroy the body, by burning a part, and throwing the remainder into the college vault. The disappearance of Dr. Parkman caused intense excitement, and efforts were made to find a trace of him, but without success, until the janitor of the college discovered the remains in the vault. Webster was immediately arrested, tried, found guilty, and executed. Before he died, he confessed that he had killed Dr. Parkman. The whole matter, from the disappearance of Dr. Parkman to the execution of Dr. Webster, created the most intense excitement all over the country.

JAIL, AND EYE AND EAR INFIRMARY.

As the car nears the bridge, the visitor will see, on the right, a short distance back from the street, a massive granite building. This is the Boston Jail. The entrance is on a side street, called North Charles Street. This building is two stories high, built upon what is known as the Auburn plan — a prison within a prison. The main building is octagonal in form, with four wings, one from the north, south, east, and west. The lower story of the main building is used as kitchen, bakery, laundry, &c. The upper story is a guard and inspection room. The wings contain the cells. The entire building is strongly and expensively constructed, and is remarkably well adapted to the purposes for which it was intended. Charles Street is the street opposite that on which the jail is situated. On the right hand side of this street, a short distance from Cambridge Street, may be seen a very neatly constructed building, of brick, called the Massachusetts Eye and Ear Infirmary. This building is under the charge of a charitable association, and is intended for the use of the poor exclusively. No fees are ever charged by the society.

CAMBRIDGE BRIDGE.

The car next approaches the West Boston Bridge, heretofore referred to as having materially contributed to the prosperity of Cambridge. In 1792, certain influential and public-spirited persons of Boston were incorporated, for the purpose of building this bridge from what was then called the Pest House, in Boston, (at some distance east of the present Boston abutment of the bridge,) to what was called Pelham's Island, near Cambridge, with a causeway thence to the Cambridge shore. The work on the causeway was commenced July 15, 1792. The wood work of the bridge was commenced April 8, 1793. The bridge and causeway were opened for passengers November 23, 1793. The bridge was 40 feet wide, and 2845 feet in length. The causeway was 3344 feet long, and the whole cost £23,000, or about $76,666. The first bridge was built upon pine wood piles, which, going rapidly to decay, were replaced by oaken ones a few years later. By the original act of incorporation, the bridge corporation was granted a toll for seventy years from the opening of the bridge. This right of toll would have expired in 1863, but it was afterwards extended to the year 1879, in consideration of the granting of a charter to the proprietors of Canal Bridge to East Cambridge, the supposition being that the erection of the latter bridge would decrease the receipts on the West Boston Bridge. The proprietors of the bridge continued to take tolls until the year 1846, although for many years previously the payment of the toll was, by the citizens of Cambridge, universally felt to be an onerous charge upon them, and, to a certain extent, was thought to retard the growth of the town. In 1846, the legislature came to the relief of the people, and passed an act authorizing the erection of the Hancock Free Bridge *between* the two bridges. The construction of this bridge, it was seen by the two old corporations, would seriously interfere with their profits, the amount of which, although small at the commencement of their enterprises, had then for many years

been excessive, and almost beyond belief. They therefore
both offered to sell their bridges to the new corporation, in
accordance with a provision in the charter of the latter.
The proposed new free bridge was therefore never erected,
but the two old bridges passed into the possession of the
new corporation, whose object was to raise, by issue of
stock, sufficient to pay for the bridges, then to raise a fund
sufficient to pay off that stock with interest, and to keep the
two bridges in repair forever ; the bridges then to become free
avenues for public travel. The amount paid for the bridges
was $135,000, — $75,000 for the West Boston, and $60,000
for the Canal Bridge. This was soon paid off; both bridges
were substantially rebuilt, the causeway laid out as a public
street, about seven hundred and fifty feet of the West Boston Bridge, principally on the Cambridge side, filled up solid,
and a fund of $100,000 raised to keep the bridges in repair.
This fund was then passed over to the city of Cambridge,
according to law, and will be held by them forever for that
purpose. On the 1st of February, 1858, the bridges were
declared free, and the event was duly celebrated by the citizens of Cambridge.

MASSACHUSETTS GENERAL HOSPITAL.

As soon as the car reaches the draw of the bridge, the
visitor will have a fine opportunity to view the jail again.
The white granite building next beyond the jail, and to the
left, facing the latter, is the Massachusetts General Hospital.
The corner stone of this building was laid July 4, 1818,
with great pomp, and the building was completed in September, 1821. The erection of the Hospital originated
from a bequest of five thousand dollars, left by a gentleman
who died towards the close of the last century, for the purpose of aiding in the erecting of a hospital. Nothing was
however done until 1810, when steps were taken towards
carrying out the wishes of the testator. In 1811 a large
number of gentlemen, interested in the subject, procured an
act of incorporation, under the name of the Massachusetts
General Hospital. That act granted to the corporation an
estate called the Old Province House, in Boston, where the
governors of the province formerly resided, and which has
since been turned into a negro concert hall. The grant
was, however, upon the condition that one hundred thousand dollars additional should be raised by subscription

within ten years. This sum was raised within a few years, soon after which the present building was erected, and an estate in Somerville purchased, for the accommodation of such insane patients whose friends were willing to pay their expenses. The insane asylum is called the McLean Asylum, from one of the largest benefactors of the hospital. The building in Boston has, within a few years, been materially . enlarged by the addition of wings.

VIEW FROM THE BRIDGE.

The visitor will now notice the Canal Bridge to East Cambridge, the next bridge to the right when facing Cambridge. This bridge has been before referred to. Bunker Hill Monument, at Charlestown, will be seen towering in the distance, a short distance from which is the State Prison, a granite building, with a cupola, directly beyond one of the circular buildings used as a locomotive engine house. Next, the tall chimney of the New England Glass Company will be seen, and then in East Cambridge, near the end of the Canal Bridge, the county buildings of the county of Middlesex, the Court House, Registry of Deeds, Probate, &c., and in front of them, the House of Correction, Jail, &c.

On the left of the bridge, the polygonal shaped building on the Boston side is an enormous gas-holder, constructed by the Boston Gas Light Company in 1858, for the purpose of storing gas made during the day, for use at night. This is but one of several gas-holders owned by the company in Boston.

The bridge next to the West Boston Bridge on this side, is what is called the Mill Dam, or Western Avenue, leading from Boston to Brookline. This is a solid structure, commenced in 1818, and finished in 1821. It is a mile and a half long, and, in some parts, a hundred feet in width. The opposite shore, between the Mill Dam and the West Boston Bridge, forms parts of the towns of Brookline, Brighton, and Cambridge.

CAMBRIDGEPORT.

There will be found nothing of interest after the bridge has been passed, until the car turns the curve near the Universalist Church, in Cambridgeport.

That part of Cambridge extending from near the church

2

to within about three quarters of a mile of the College buildings, is what is usually called Cambridgeport. That part of the city immediately beyond the bridge has usually been denominated the "Lower Port." This latter part of the city seemed at one time destined to become an important business place. It was one of the first enterprises after the adoption of the constitution of the United States, "and its successful progress in the outset was in accordance with the prosperity of the country under the impulses given to it by the first administration of the new government." Several large stores were erected there, a tavern was built, "and in a few years quite a handsome village sprang up, in a manner quite novel in that age." Roads, wharves, and canals were constructed at a great expense, to meet the expected trade, the place was made a port of delivery by Congress, plans were drawn of an embryo town, which contained reservations for court building, markets, &c., and every thing seemed to show that Cambridgeport would soon become a thriving place. "But competitors soon arose, in the form of new improvements, which attracted the public mind, and drew away the nourishment that sustained Cambridgeport, and dispersed it among numbers of hungry claimants. West Boston Bridge brought into existence Cambridgeport, and before it had time for any substantial maturity, clouds and darkness portended its fate. South Boston, Canal Bridge, and the Mill Dam followed in rapid succession, all expecting to derive their support from the same source which had cherished the little settlement of Cambridgeport — the trade of the county, and the sale of lands to actual settlers." Then came the embargo, which "palsied the energies of this thrifty village," and "thus ended the first splendid race of competition in the suburbs of Boston."

City Hall.

After passing the Universalist Church at the curve, the visitor fairly enters Cambridgeport. The first object of interest is the City Hall, a large brick building (a cut of which we give) at the left, a short distance beyond the church. This structure was erected for the use of the Cambridge Athenæum, and was, in 1858, sold to the city for a City Hall. Thomas Dowse, formerly well known as a resident of this part of the city, left by will a large sum of money, to be expended by his executors for charitable and

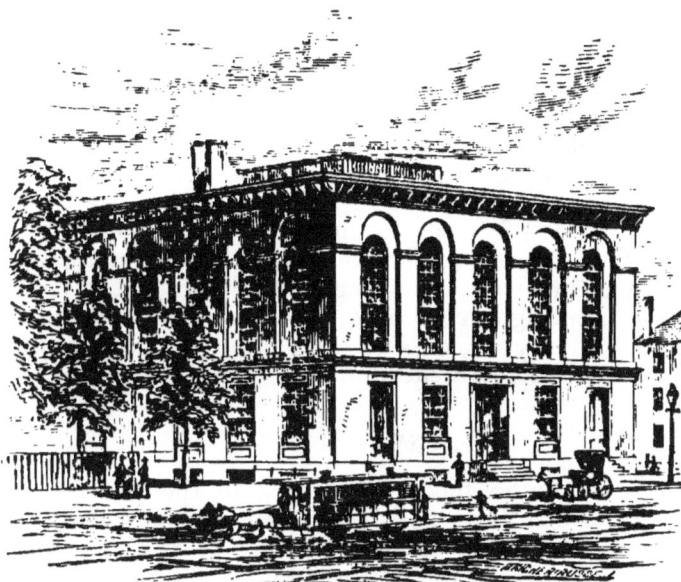

CITY HALL, CAMBRIDGEPORT.

See page 14.

literary purposes. Of this amount, ten thousand dollars
were paid to the city in 1858, for the purpose of sustaining a
course of public lectures in the large and beautiful hall in
the second story of this building. The lower story is used
for the public offices. The land on which the building
stands was a gift from Edmund T. Dana. The city paid
fifteen thousand dollars for the estate and personal property
connected therewith, including the Athenæum Library, Mr.
Dana consenting to the transfer, on condition that the city
should, for six years, expend three hundred dollars annually
toward the improvement of the library.

Inman House.

There is no other object of interest to the stranger, after
passing the City Hall, and before reaching the Colleges, excepting the Inman House, which is at a little distance beyond the City Hall, and on the right. It is at the corner of
Main and Inman Streets, and is a large wooden building,
standing far back from the street, with a spacious and
beautiful lawn in front. This building was built before the
revolutionary war, and was owned by Ralph Inman, a tory,
who was unceremoniously dispossessed of his property. The
building is remarkable on account of having been the head
quarters of General Israel Putnam, while the American
army was encamped at Cambridge, during the siege of
Boston.

The lofty towers of Gore Hall next appear in sight among
the College buildings on the right.

Apthorp's Palace.

We will leave Gore Hall for the present to notice a large
wooden building standing back from the side of the street
opposite that on which Gore Hall appears. This building is
to this day called the "Bishop's Palace." It was erected by
Mr. Apthorp, a gentleman of wealth, born in Boston, but
who had been educated in England. The popular belief
was, that he expected the appointment of Bishop of New
England from the English government, and intended to make
this building his official residence. He was disappointed,
however ; but the building yet remains, with traces of that
former elegance which was the wonder of the good people
of Cambridge, at the time of its erection. The British Gen-

GORE HALL (COLLEGE LIBRARY.)

See pages 16 and 18.

eral Burgoyne resided here for some time as a prisoner of war.

HARVARD COLLEGE.

Harvard College has before been referred to in general terms. The visitor can now, if he chooses, leave the car, and enjoy a stroll through the College grounds. The situation of the various buildings, or halls, as they are called, will very readily be ascertained by reference to the accompanying plan.

Gore Hall, before referred to, contains the College library. The building is of rough Quincy granite, and was erected in 1838. It is in the form of a Latin cross, the extreme length being 140 feet externally, and through the transept 81 feet. The interior contains a hall 112 feet long, 35 feet high, with a vaulted ceiling, supported by twenty ribbed columns. The spaces between the columns and side walls are divided into alcoves, above and below a gallery. There are about seventy thousand volumes in the building, a collection of Greek and Oriental manuscripts, and a large collection of coins and medals. This building is named after the Hon. Christopher Gore, who bequeathed one hundred thousand dollars to the College.

The Dane Law School was erected in 1832, with funds contributed by the Hon. Nathan Dane, after whom it is named. This building is one of the most appropriately constructed of all the College buildings.

The long row of brick buildings in Harvard Square, opposite the Law School, is called *Graduates' Hall.* The upper stories are devoted to the use of graduates, and the ground floor is leased for various business purposes. These buildings were erected in the year 1832.

Massachusetts Hall, built in 1720, is the oldest of the College buildings. It is of brick, 100 feet long, and 41 wide, and contains rooms for the use of the students.

University Hall was erected in 1814. The outer walls are composed of Chelmsford granite. This edifice contains the chapel, lecture rooms, &c. Its dimensions are, length 140 feet, width 50 feet, height 42 feet.

Harvard Hall is a large brick building erected in 1766, 108 feet long, 40 feet wide, and 38 feet in height. It was erected at the expense of the State, to replace a building of the same name, which was burned in the winter of 1764-5, while occupied by the General Court, which had removed

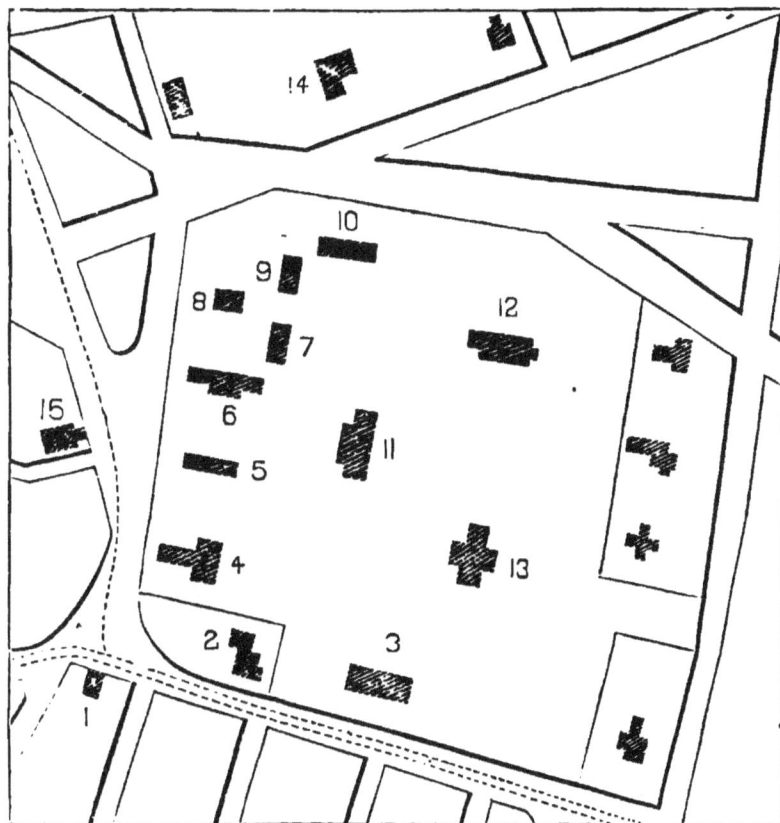

REFERENCES.

1. Railroad Station.
2. Dwelling House, formerly occupied by the President.
3. Boylston Hall.
4. Law School.
5. Massachusetts Hall.
6. Harvard Hall.
7. Hollis Hall.
8. Holden Chapel.
9. Stoughton Hall.
10. Holworthy Hall
11. University Hall.
12. Appleton Chapel.
13. Gore Hall.
14. Lawrence Scientific School.
15. Unitarian Church.

The Dotted Lines represent the Horse Railroad.

from Boston on account of the prevalence there of the small pox. The library was contained in the old building, and was destroyed, with the exception of such books as had been loaned. The present building formerly contained the library in the second story, and below had a chapel and lecture room. When the library was removed to Gore Hall, the lower story was remodelled, and now consists of a single room, where the Alumni dine on Commencement. Around it are hung the portraits of the benefactors of the College, many of them works of the first painters of the day. The mineralogical cabinet is above, and is a very fine collection. It contains the most perfect specimen of the skeleton of the mastodon ever discovered. The College bell is upon Harvard Hall.

Hollis Hall contains rooms for the students. It was erected in 1763, and is built of brick. It is 105 feet in length, 44 in breadth, and 37 in height. It was named after the Hollis family, several members of which were very large benefactors of the College.

Holden Chapel was erected in 1744, and is of brick. The funds for its erection were contributed by the widow and daughters of Samuel Holden, a merchant of London, who died a few years before its erection. This building was long used as a chapel, but is now devoted to medical purposes, and contains a large anatomical museum.

Stoughton Hall was built in 1805. It is of brick, and is devoted to the use of the students. It was named after William Stoughton, who was lieutenant governor and chief justice of the province.

Holworthy Hall, named after Sir Matthew Holworthy, a great benefactor of the College, who died in 1678, is also a brick building, erected in 1812, 138 feet long, 34 in breadth, and 37 in height. It is occupied by the students of the senior class.

Boylston Hall was erected in 1857. It is a rough granite building, nearly in front of Gore Hall. It contains the lecture rooms of the professors of chemistry and comparative anatomy, with a laboratory and museum. Near Boylston Hall is the building, still owned by the college, and formerly occupied by the presidents. It was built in 1726.

The *Appleton Chapel* is a large freestone building, erected in 1858, from funds bequeathed by the Hon. Samuel Appleton.

Divinity Hall is very pleasantly located on Divinity Hall

Avenue, leading from Kirkland Street. It was erected in 1826, for the use of the divinity students. It is a brick ·building.

The *Lawrence Scientific School* stands on Kirkland Street. This is an uncommonly handsome brick building, devoted to the purposes of the Scientific School, founded by Abbott Lawrence, in 1848. In this school, young men, whether they have or have not received a classical education, can be taught the various scientific branches.

The *Observatory* is on an eminence at the left. It contains one of the best refracting telescopes in the world, which has contributed materially to many important discoveries in the solar system. The instrument was purchased with funds contributed by various wealthy gentlemen of Boston and vicinity. The building also contains all the instruments necessary for examinations of the stars, and for magnetic and meteorological purposes.

There is, at a short distance from the College buildings, on Linnæan Street, a Botanical Garden, seven acres in extent, under the charge of the professor of botany. This garden, first established in 1807, is laid out in an ornamental style, and is well furnished with an interesting collection of native and foreign trees, shrubs, and plants.

The government of the College is vested in a corporation, consisting of the president, treasurer, and five fellows, a board of overseers composed of the president of the college, the governor and lieutenant governor of the state, the members of the state executive council, and the senate, together with the speaker of the house of representatives, and thirty other gentlemen, (fifteen clergymen resident in Boston and vicinity, and fifteen laymen,) elected by the legislature. The faculty of instruction, embracing the professional and scientific schools, consists of the president, twenty-eight professors, five tutors, and several teachers. The degree of bachelor of arts is conferred at the close of a course of four years' study. The term of study in the Divinity School is three years, and in the Law School three years. The medical lectures are delivered in the Medical College in Boston.

Harvard College, as has been remarked, is the most richly endowed of all the colleges in the country. It received many benefactions from wealthy persons in England before the revolution, and both before and since that time, has received large sums from the state and private individuals. Recent contributions have been almost altogether from private citizens.

The church in the square opposite the railroad station is that of the Old Cambridge Baptist society. The church on the left, opposite the College buildings, is the Unitarian Church, in which the exercises are held on Commencement Day. Several of the Presidents of the College were buried in the graveyard adjoining this church. The wooden building with a circular end, near the Baptist Church, at the left, belongs to the College, and is used for a music hall.

Nearly opposite the college buildings is the Common, near the north-westerly corner of which is the famous Washington Elm. Beneath this tree General Washington first drew his sword as commander-in-chief of the American army, on the morning of July 3, 1775.

BRATTLE HOUSE.

The visitor should now reënter the cars, and proceed on the road to Mount Auburn. The Brattle House will soon be passed. This building was erected for a hotel, but the speculation proved a disastrous one to the originators, and the building was afterwards sold to the College authorities, and is now principally occupied by the law students.

MR. LONGFELLOW'S RESIDENCE.

Some very beautiful residences will now be passed, on both sides of the road, which will attract the attention of the visitor. On the right will be seen a large wooden house, painted yellow, with white, ornamental columns. This building is supposed to have been erected by Colonel John Vassal, who died in 1747. It fell by descent to his son John, who was a noted royalist. It then became the head quarters of General Washington, during the siege of Boston. It was afterwards owned by Thomas Tracy, Joseph Lee, and Andrew Craigie, after whom it was called the Craigie House, and is now owned by Henry Wadsworth Longfellow, the poet. The room upon the lower floor, at the right of the door, was occupied as a study by General Washington, and is now used for the same purpose by Mr. Longfellow. The room over it was occupied by the general as a sleeping room. The room in the rear of the study was occupied by the aids-de-camp, and is now used as a library room. The poet's own lines refer, on several occasions, to the associations connected with the Craigie House. In his "Lines to a Child," it is thus referred to : —

MR. LONGFELLOW'S RESIDENCE.

See page 22.

" Once, ah, once, within these walls,
One whom memory oft recalls,
    The Father of his Country, dwelt,
And yonder meadows broad and damp,
The fires of the besieging camp
    Encircled with a burning belt.
Up and down these echoing stairs,
Heavy with the weight of cares,
    Sounded his majestic tread ;
Yes, within this very room,
Sat he in those hours of gloom,
    Weary both in heart and head."

RIEDESEL HOUSE.

At a short distance above Mr. Longfellow's residence, at
the corner of Sparks Street, may be seen the house in which
the Brunswick general, Baron Riedesel, and his family were
quartered, during the stay of the captive army of Burgoyne
in the vicinity of Boston.   This house may be recognized
by the large number of beautiful linden trees around it.
On a pane of one of the windows may still be seen the name
of the baroness, supposed to have been engraved thereon by
herself, with the diamond of her ring.   The house is now
occupied by John Brewster, Esq.

DR. LOWELL'S RESIDENCE.

At the south-west corner of Elmwood Avenue is the
estate of the Rev. Dr. Lowell.   The house, almost entirely
concealed from view by trees, was erected by the famous
Andrew Oliver, the stamp commissioner, who was hung in
effigy by the people of Boston in 1765, and whose stamp
office, or rather a building supposed to be intended for a
stamp office, was destroyed by a mob.   Oliver was at his
house in Cambridge at the time, and was waited upon by
the mob, but they departed without doing him any injury.
Oliver being a refugee, the estate was confiscated, and while
the American army was quartered at Cambridge in 1775,
the house was used as a hospital.   Several soldiers must
have been buried near the house, for when Mount Auburn
Street was graded, a few years since, a large number of
skeletons was found that had evidently been in graves.   The
estate was afterwards owned by Elbridge Gerry, a signer of
the Declaration of Independence, a governor of Massachusetts, and, the time of his death, Vice President of the
United States.

MOUNT AUBURN CEMETERY.

In the year 1831, the Massachusetts Horticultural Society, of which Joseph Story, the late eminent jurist, was president, obtained from the legislature of the state an act authorizing them "to dedicate and appropriate" any part of the real estate then owned or to be afterwards purchased by them, "as and for a rural cemetery or burying ground." The ground selected for the purpose is the present Cemetery, enlarged by successive purchases to 126½ acres. It was named, from its principal eminence, Mount Auburn, which is one hundred and twenty-five feet above the level of Charles River. A tower, sixty feet high, has since been erected on this mount, from the top of which can be obtained one of the finest prospects in the environs of Boston. The grounds were consecrated on the 24th of September, 1831. A temporary amphitheatre was erected in a part of the grounds called "Consecration Dell," a deep, picturesque valley, with a platform for the speakers at the bottom. The services consisted of instrumental music; an introductory prayer, by the Rev. Henry Ware, Jr.; an original hymn, by the Rev. John Pierpont, sung by the audience; an address, by Judge Story; and a concluding prayer, by Mr. Pierpont. The following is the hymn written by the latter: —

"To thee, O God, in humble trust,
    Our hearts their cheerful incense burn,
For this thy word, 'Thou art of dust,'
    And unto dust shalt thou return.

"And what were life, life's work all done,
    The hopes, joys, loves, that cling to clay?
All, all departed, one by one,
    And yet life's load borne on for aye!

"Decay! decay! 'tis stamped on all;
    All bloom in flower and flesh shall fade;
Ye whispering trees, when ye shall fall,
    Be our long sleep beneath your shade!

"Here to thy bosom, Mother Earth,
    Take back in peace what thou hast given,
And all that is of heavenly birth,
    O God, in peace recall to heaven."

3

A writer in a magazine published at that time thus describes the scene at the consecration : —

"An unclouded sun, and an atmosphere purified by the showers of the preceding night, combined to make the day one of the most beautiful ever experienced at that delightful season of the year. The perfect silence of the multitude enabled the several speakers to be heard with perfect distinctness at the remotest part of the amphitheatre. The effect produced by the music of the thousand voices which united in the hymn, as it swelled in chastened melody from the bottom and sides of the glen, and, like the spirit of devotion, found an echo in every heart, and pervaded the whole scene, we cannot attempt to describe. It is believed that in the course of a few years, when the hand of Taste shall have passed over the luxuriance of Nature, we may challenge the rivalry of the world to produce another such abiding place for the spirit of beauty. It has now become holy ground, — a village of the quick and the silent, where Nature throws an air of cheerfulness over the labors of Death. To what better place can we go with the musing of sadness, or for the indulgence of grief? where to cool the burning brow of ambition, or relieve the swelling heart of disappointment? We can find no better spot for the rambles of curiosity, health, or pleasure; none sweeter, for the whispers of affection among the loving; none holier, for the last rest of our kindred.

"If there be any wisdom to be gathered among the tombs, any useful though hard lessons to be learned there, is it profitable to place cemeteries where they will seldom be entered by either the thoughtless, the reflecting, the gay, or the grave? Who would richly endow a school, and place it where a pupil would seldom come? A tomb is, it has been said, a monument on the limits of both worlds; it is a tower on the narrow isthmus that separates life from death, and time from eternity; and standing upon it, we look back with double regret on the misprized and misspent past, and renew our failing resolutions for the dark and boundless future. 'Shadows, clouds, and darkness rest upon it;' it is but natural to strive after more perfection, and to feel the better hopes of hereafter, when surrounded by the graves of good men who have gone before.

'Tully was not so eloquent as thou,
Thou nameless pillar with the broken base.'

Mount Auburn, too, will have its own persuasive eloquence."

In memory of the day of consecration, the following stanzas were written soon after by Charles Sprague, Esq. : —

" There was a garden, and in the garden a new sepulchre."

"What myriads throng, in proud array,
  With songs of joy and flags unfurled,
To consecrate the glorious day
  That gave a nation to the world!

"We raise no shout, no trumpet sound,
  No banner to the breeze we spread ;
Children of clay ! bend humbly round ;
  We plant a city to the dead.

"For man a garden rose in bloom,
  When yon glad sun began to burn ;
He fell, and heard the awful doom, —
  'Of dust thou art ; to dust return !'

"But HE in whose pure faith we come,
  Who in a gloomier garden lay,
Assured us of a brighter home,
  And rose, and led the glorious way.

"HIS word we trust ! When life shall end,
  Here be our long, long slumber passed ;
To the *first* garden's doom we bend,
  And bless the promise of the *last*."

The Massachusetts Horticultural Society were proprietors of the Cemetery grounds until the incorporation of the "Proprietors of the Cemetery of Mount Auburn," in the year 1835, when all the rights of the former society to the premises were transferred to the present proprietors. By the act of incorporation, every person owning a lot in the Cemetery, containing three hundred square feet, is a member of the corporation. Meetings of the proprietors are held annually, for choice of officers for the management of the funds, and care of the grounds. The affairs of the corporation are at present managed by a board of twelve trustees, a treasurer, secretary, superintendent, and gate keeper.

The present price of ordinary lots in the Cemetery is at the rate of fifty cents per square foot. The lots usually contain about three hundred square feet. Choice lots are held at advanced prices.

The funds received from the sales of lots are devoted to the care of the grounds, to beautify and adorn the Cemetery, and to form a reserve fund, which shall accumulate, and the interest of which shall be used at some future time, when the wants of the corporation require it, for the payment of its expenses. Proprietors, it is expected, will keep their own lots in order, and the fences and monuments in repair, but the corporation will receive from any proprietor a sum of money to be agreed upon, and will give a guarantee that the lot or lots of such proprietor shall be kept in perpetual repair. To every proprietor is given a ticket entitling him and his household to drive with a carriage into the grounds. These tickets are not transferable. Strangers can obtain special tickets to allow them to drive into the Cemetery with a carriage, by applying to one of the officers of the corporation. The Cemetery gates are open from sunrise to sunset every day, excepting Sundays and holidays, for the free admission of the public on foot. No one but a proprietor, or person bearing a ticket of admission, will be allowed to enter the Cemetery with a vehicle. The Cemetery gates are closed on Sundays and holidays to the public, but a proprietor can obtain admission on presenting his ticket. Relatives or near friends of persons interred within the Cemetery can also obtain admittance on Sundays or holidays, on presenting a ticket, to be obtained of one of the officers of the corporation.

Certain regulations have been adopted by the trustees, to be observed by visitors to the Cemetery, which may be read at length posted in various places within the grounds.

Before the visitor enters the Cemetery, the gateway will naturally attract his attention. This gateway was built of solid Quincy granite; the design was taken from the entrance to an Egyptian temple. It bears the following inscription : —

THEN SHALL THE DUST RETURN TO THE EARTH AS IT WAS : AND THE SPIRIT SHALL RETURN UNTO GOD WHO GAVE IT.

Eccles. xii. 7.

The visitor is now supposed to enter the Cemetery.

" With thy rude ploughshare, Death, turn up the sod,
    And spread the furrow for the seed we sow ;
    This is the field and Acre of our God,
    This is the place where human harvests grow."

On the interior of the gateway is inscribed —

MOUNT AUBURN, CONSECRATED SEPTEMBER 24, 1831.

We propose now to lay out a ROUTE through the Cemetery, by following which the visitor will be enabled to view the most prominent and interesting monuments, and to visit the most attractive points in the grounds. By following this route, there will be fine opportunities to view the Spurzheim, Bowditch, C. J. F. Binney, Magoun, Knight, Richardson, Appleton, Amos Binney, Kirkland, Ossoli, Thayer, Ashmun, Appleton, Murray, Hannah Adams, Whiting, Buckingham, Story, Webster, Winchester, Bigelow, Perkins, Tisdale and Hewins, Story, Allen, Lawrence, and many other monuments and lots that attract notice, not only from the associations connected with the names they bear, but also on account of the refined taste exhibited in the designs, and the beauty displayed in the execution. The route, as here laid down, shows the visitor to the Chapel, the Tower, to Harvard Hill, the burying place of persons connected with the College; it shows them the way to Juniper, Cedar, and Pine Hills, and also to Central Square, and leads them directly, not only to the borders of Meadow, Forest, and Garden Ponds, but also to the celebrated Consecration Dell, where the ceremonies of consecration were performed, September 24, 1831. As we pass along this route, we shall notice the more prominent monuments and lots, and when possible, without exceeding our limits, shall give the inscriptions on the most interesting monuments, in full. We shall not, however, enter upon any architectural descriptions of the various monuments, nor indulge in any remarks concerning the want of good taste that may *seem* to have been exhibited in the arrangement of any of the lots, the designs of any of the various memorials, or in the selection of some of the inscriptions. Want of space will forbid the one, and our own sense of propriety the other. Our object is not to describe Mount Auburn as any one thinks it *should be*, but to lead the visitor through the most interesting portions of the Cemetery, to call the attention to every thing on the route worthy of observation, and thus enable him to view Mount Auburn *as it is* — as Nature, Art, and Affection have made it.

For those visitors who do not desire to accompany us in our description of the grounds, but only wish to avail themselves of our proposed route, we have prepared the following condensed directions, which are the same as those to be given in succeeding pages with the descriptions.

3 *

Visitors who desire to see the grounds and monuments from the best possible points of view, should follow strictly the Directions.

Central Avenue, it should be remembered, is the principal avenue in the Cemetery, and leads *directly* to the Gate. The route crosses Central Avenue several times. Visitors, therefore, who do not desire to go through the entire route, can, after having passed over a portion of the route, and again reached Central Avenue, return directly to the Gate.

DIRECTIONS.

Wherever the Directions do not appear to be perfectly distinct, a reference to the Plan will put the visitor right. The route is marked very distinctly upon the Plan.

1. Pass through Central Avenue, and turn to the right into Chapel Avenue.

2. Pass through Chapel Avenue to the Chapel.

3. Enter the Chapel, and, after having left it, continue on in the same path as before, and turn to the right into Pine Avenue.

4. Pass through Pine Avenue, and turn to the left into Yarrow Path, passing around the Homer lot, No. 1321.

5. Pass through Yarrow Path, and turn to the right into Fir Avenue.

6. Pass through Fir Avenue a short distance, and turn to the left into Elm Avenue.

7. Pass through Elm Avenue, and turn to the left into Mistletoe Path.

8. Pass through Mistletoe Path, and turn to the left into Greenbrier Path — the first path on the left.

9. Pass through Greenbrier Path, and turn to the right into Fir Avenue.

10. Pass through Fir Avenue, turn to the left into Heliotrope Path, view the Gardner monument on the left, and then return to Fir Avenue.

11. Pass through Fir Avenue, and turn to the left into Columbine Path.

12. Pass through Columbine Path, examine the Binney and Thayer monuments on the right, then pass between the two lots, and turn to the right into Heath Path.

13. Pass through Heath Path, and turn to the left again into Fir Avenue.

14. Pass through Fir Avenue, and turn to the left into Spruce Avenue.

15. Pass through Spruce Avenue as far as Heliotrope Path, there examine the Allen monument, then return, and turn to the left into Eglantine Path.

16. Pass through Eglantine Path, then turn to the left, pass between the Pierce lot, No. 991, and the Bagley lot, No. 1539, and turn to the right into Cypress Avenue.

17. Pass through Cypress Avenue until the St. James public lot, No. 82, is reached; pass through the path nearly opposite the centre of the front of that lot, and then turn to the left into Hibiscus Path, the second path on the left.

18. Pass through Hibiscus Path, and turn to the right into Cypress Avenue.

19. Pass through Cypress Avenue, and turn to the right into Central Avenue.

20. Pass through Central Avenue, turn to the left, pass through the narrow path, upon which the Gray and Prince tombs front, and then turn to the right into Geranium Path.

21. Pass through Geranium Path, and turn to the right into Beech Avenue.

22. Pass through Beech Avenue toward Central Square; go around the square, to the left; pass between the Knight lot, No. 662, on the right, and the Smith lot, No. 48, on the left; pass in front of the Murray monument, No. 587, and through a narrow path at the right, passing near the Dana lot, No. 1373; then turn to the left into Walnut Avenue.

23. Pass through Walnut Avenue, turn to the right, and pass around the Field lot, No. 169, into Pyrola Path.

24. Pass through Pyrola Path; turn to the left, and pass around the Dehon lot, No. 1337, into Bellwort Path; then cross over again in the same way into Trefoil Path, the next path beyond, and then turn to the left.

25. Pass through Trefoil Path a short distance, and then turn into Tulip Path, the first path on the right.

26. Pass through Tulip Path, and turn to the right into Walnut Avenue.

27. Pass through Walnut Avenue, and turn to the left into Mountain Avenue, to the Tower.

28. After having ascended to the top of the Tower, descend and go around the structure, and turn into Hazel Path near two large granite obelisks on the Fuller lot.

29. Pass through Hazel Path, passing the Farnum tomb,

c

No. 184, on the left, then turn to the right, and pass across Harvard Hill; pass the Kirkland monument and the Ashmun monument. After viewing the latter, keep to the left, and descend the hill; pass in front of the Fuller tomb, on Woodbine Path; then ascend Cedar Hill, and pass alongside of the Appleton monument, a beautiful white marble temple, of which we give a cut, and from near which Consecration Dell may be seen at the left; then continue almost in a straight line, slightly inclined to the right, however, and descend the hill and enter Lily Path.

30. Pass through Lily Path, and turn to the right into Hemlock Path, the first path on the right.

31. Pass through Hemlock Path, and turn to the left into Willow Avenue, the second path on the left.

32. Pass through Willow Avenue, and turn to the left into Narcissus Path.

33. Pass through Narcissus Path, on the left side of Forest Pond, and then, keeping to the right, turn into Alder Path.

34. Pass through Alder Path, turn to the right into Locust Avenue, and again to the right into Beech Avenue.

35. Pass through Beech Avenue, and turn to the right into Linden Path.

36. Pass through Linden Path, and then continue on, almost in a straight line into Catalpa Path.

37. Pass through Catalpa Path, and then continue on, keeping to the left into Indian Ridge Path.

38. Pass through Indian Ridge Path, which terminates in Central Avenue.

39. Pass through Central Avenue to the Gate.

THE ROUTE IN THE CEMETERY.

CENTRAL AVENUE.

Pass down Central Avenue. The first monument seen is that of Gaspar Spurzheim, the celebrated phrenologist, born Dec. 31, 1775, died in Boston, Nov. 10, 1832, aged 57. This monument is of white marble, is on an eminence at the left, and will readily attract the visitor's attention. It is beautifully designed and executed, and is inclosed with an ornamented circular railing. This was one of the earliest erected monuments in the Cemetery.

SPURZHEIM MONUMENT.
See page 32.

The Goddard monument on the right will next attract attention, and then that erected to the memory of **Gedney King**, beyond. The Willis lot on the left contains a monument of a very neat and appropriate design, the lot being inclosed by an iron fence, also of a very appropriate design. The lot of George H. Jones on the right will be particularly noticed as containing, at the side of the large monument, two smaller figures, male and female. Under the latter is the word NOT, and under the other SEPARATED. The Goddard monument at the right will next be noticed. This is a neatly ornamented column, with an urn at the top, encircled with a wreath of flowers. *Turn to the right, and pass into Chapel Avenue.*

CHAPEL AVENUE.

At the visitor's left hand will be seen the celebrated *bronze* statue of Dr. Nathaniel Bowditch. This statue represents Dr. Bowditch calmly seated with a globe and quadrant at his feet, his right arm resting upon a book. The statue was designed by Ball Hughes, and was cast in Boston at the foundery of Messrs. Gooding and Gavett. It was the first full length bronze statue ever cast in this country, the Franklin statue in front of the City Hall, Boston, being the second.

Dr. Bowditch is known as the author of the "American Practical Navigator," the translator of the first four volumes of "Méchanique Céleste," and as author of various other scientific communications, memoirs, &c. A memoir of his life has been published, and to it we refer those who desire to gain further information concerning one whose "name," as Mr. Quincy, in his History of Harvard University, says, "became, before his death, identified with the loftiest branches of science, and united indissolubly with those of Newton and La Place." Dr. Bowditch was born in Salem, Mass., March 26, 1773, and died in Boston March 6, 1838.

The statue was erected over the tomb of Dr. Bowditch in 1847. When it was on its way to the Cemetery, it was carried, at the hour of high 'Change, to State Street, Boston, where it remained for some time, gazed upon by many who had known the living subject. The incident called forth the following anonymous lines published in one of our papers of the day : —

BRONZE STATUE OF DR. NATHANIEL BOWDITCH.

See pages 34 and 35

THE BRONZE STATUE.

Friends and neighbors, cease your traffic ! What is this comes passing
 near,
Heavy, o'er the groaning pavement, moving slowly like a bier?
Lo ! it seems the sculptured semblance of an old and reverend man :
Bid them stop a while before us : let us all the features scan.
Well we knew him — yes ! we knew him ; — see his high and massive
 brow !
But how solemn looks he sitting ! meditating seems he now.
Yes, those firm and solemn features — fall the night and rise the morn -
Shall be seen by mortal vision when a thousand years are gone.
 Tell us thou how runs his story, while we contemplate its end ;
Thou whose hoary head bespeaks thee friend and comrade of our friend.
" Child of this our great Republic, brother of the toiling poor,
Slight assistance gained his labors from the Wealthy's golden store.
But his reasoning tracked the mazes where abstrusest science dwelt ;
Early he, an earnest pilgrim, at the feet of Knowledge knelt.
Then we saw him, as a seaman, gain and learning seek to reap ;
Thinking, as he ploughed the ocean ; studying, on the roaring deep.
Unsought honors beckoned to him, foreign lands proclaimed his worth,
And they named the learned sailor 'mongst the honored ones of earth.
Many tongues he spake and studied ; gauged the fiery meteor's mass ;
And expounded to the people where the blazing comets pass.
Fresher wreaths he gave his country ; not the warrior's bloody bays,
But the glory which the century to the ' man of uses ' pays.
Failings had he — he was mortal ; friends, he numbered many a one ;
Turn your eyes upon the statue, for my tale is nearly done.
Full of years, he closed his eyelids, softly drew his dying breath,
And the flags of many nations waved at half-mast on his death."
 Sits the form like Archimedes, in his closet as he staid,
Solving earnestly his problem, heedless of the Roman blade.
Messenger to unknown futures, reflex of our age and clime,
Leader of a stately phalanx, lengthening down the road of time ;
Rising now there comes before me visions of the glorious day,
When the veil that blinds the people, rent in rags, shall float away.
O, my nation ! free and fearless, may thy future glory be
To count amongst thy sons of labor many millions such as he.

  *   *   *   *   *   *   *

Place the statue on the hillock, where we laid his bones, alas !
Leave it there until he rises. Back ! and let the statue pass.

In the rear of the Bowditch statue may be seen a broken
column erected on the Coleman lot, with the hour-glass and
other emblems sculptured upon it.

Behind the Coleman monument there is a marble cenotaph, erected by the officers of the United States Exploring
Expedition to the memory of departed comrades. It bears
the following inscription : —

To the memory of Lieutenant Joseph A. Underwood and Midshipman
Wilkes Henry, U. S. N. To the memory of Passed Midshipmen Jas.
W. E. Reid and Frederick A. Bacon, U. S. N. This cenotaph is erected by their associates, the officers and scientific corps of the U. S. Exploring Expedition. Lieutenant Underwood and Midshipman Henry
fell by the hands of savages, while promoting the cause of science and
philanthropy, at Malolo, one of the Fiji Group of Islands, July 24, 1840.
Passed Midshipmen Reid and Bacon were lost at sea, off Cape Horn,
May, 1839.

DR. SHARP'S MONUMENT
See Page 38.

4

At the right of the Bowditch statue the lot of Messrs. Little and Brown will be noticed.   This lot attracts attention from the peculiar appropriateness of the design of its two freestone Gothic monuments, and the care that is evidently bestowed upon the lot itself.   Every thing about it looks neat and in good taste, and devoid of any attempt at display.   The original owners of this lot were partners in the well-known publishing house of Little, Brown & Co., of Boston.   The remains of Mr. Brown rest near the monument bearing his name.   Simple headstones mark the place of burial of members of the two familes.

The monument erected to the memory of Dr. Sharp, late pastor of the Baptist Church in Charles Street, will next be seen upon the left side of the avenue.   It is an exceedingly ornate structure, and attracts considerable attention from the peculiarity of its design.   It bears the following inscription : —

To the Rev. Daniel Sharp, D. D.; born in Huddersfield, Yorkshire, England, Dec. 25, 1783 ; died at Stoneleigh, near Baltimore, Maryland, June 23, 1853, in the seventieth year of his age.

On the reverse side is the following : —

To the Rev. Daniel Sharp, D. D., Pastor of the Charles Street Baptist Church and Society, Boston, from April 29, 1812, to June 23, 1853. The love and veneration of his people, and the wide-felt respect with which he was honored beyond the circle of his official labors, have prompted the erection of this monument.

The Lawrence inclosure on the left is, to every visitor, one of the most attractive in the Cemetery.   There are six ordinary-sized lots inclosed within the railing, each of which is owned by one of the members of this well-known family of Boston merchants.   The tall marble column upon a massive marble pedestal on the lot at the left is to the memory of

Abbott Lawrence, born at Groton, Massachusetts, Dec. 16, 1792 ; died at Boston, August 18, 1855.

The column is surmounted by an urn partially covered with drapery.   This monument was designed and executed by Joseph Carew.   On one of the rear lots is a tablet

In memory of Amos Lawrence, who was born in Groton, April 22, 1786 ; died in Boston, Dec. 31, 1852.

> Servant of God, well done ;
>   Rest from thy loved employ ;
> The battle fought, the victory won,
>   Enter thy Master's joy.
>
> The voice at midnight came ;
>   He started up to hear ;

LAWRENCE MONUMENT.

See page 38.

A mortal arrow pierced his frame ;
He fell — but felt no fear.

There is also a monument within the inclosure

To the memory of William Lawrence; born in Groton, Sept. 7,
1783 ; died in Boston, Oct. 14, 1848. The memory of the just is blessed.

There are in the inclosure several smaller tablets to the
memory of other members of the family.

The Chapel.

The visitor will shortly reach the Chapel. This edifice is
of granite, and of a Gothic design. It was erected for the
purpose of affording a suitable place for funeral services,
and for the reception of statues and other pieces of delicate
sculpture unfit to bear exposure to the air of our variable
climate. There are at present two statues of marble in the
building ; one of Joseph Story, the late eminent jurist, and
first President of the Proprietors of Mount Auburn, executed by his son, and the other of John Winthrop, first
Governor of Massachusetts, executed by Richard Greenough.
Both of these statues are in a sitting posture. Two other
statues are to be added hereafter ; one of John Adams, second President of the United States, and the other of James
Otis, the American patriot. This Chapel is the second
erected upon the spot. The first was built in 1848, but
after having been erected a few months, began to show
signs of decay. The atmosphere acted upon the stone of the
outer walls, and rapidly decomposed and stained it, owing
to the fact that it contained iron. It soon became necessary
to remove the structure ; this was done, and the present
building was erected in its place. The new Chapel is very
nearly a copy of the old one. Opposite to the entrance to
the Chapel there is a beautiful ornamental lot belonging to
the corporation, which is kept in most excellent order.

*After having left the Chapel, continue on in the same path as
before, and turn to the right into Pine Avenue.*

Pine Avenue.

On the left is the Shaw lot, containing a very appropriate
freestone temple, on which is inscribed, —

Robert Gould Shaw. 1843.

There is a white marble slab in front of the temple,
beautifully sculptured in relief. Next to the Shaw lot is
the Trull lot, with an appropriate marble monument to
the memory of

Mary Trull, died June 10, 1856, aged 70 years.

THE CHAPEL.

On the right are three very tall columns — W. H. Delano and W. F. Whitney, both of granite, and H. T. Rice, of marble. These are inclosed in a triple lot, and are exceedingly appropriate, but plain, and attract considerable attention. On the left are monuments on the Thayer, Viles, and Dodd lots, and on the right a monument of marble, with a female figure resting on an urn, inscribed, —

My Husband ;

erected to the memory of Charles Valentine.

Died Jan. 10, 1850, aged 52 years, 10 months.

This life's a dream ; an empty show ;
But the bright world to which I go
Hath joys substantial and sincere ;
When shall I wake and find me there ?

On the left is the Wetherell lot, and behind it a most beautiful granite obelisk, erected by Thomas Dowse to the memory of Franklin, and bearing the following upon its front : —

To the memory of Benjamin Franklin, the Printer, the Philosopher, the Statesman, the Patriot, who by his wisdom blessed his country and his age, and bequeathed to the world an illustrious example of industry, integrity, and self-culture. Born in Boston, MDCCVI. ; died in Philadelphia, MDCCXC.

The lot upon which the Franklin monument stands is on Gentian Path, and immediately in front of that monument is one of similar construction, but smaller, erected by Mr. Dowse over his own tomb. Mr. Dowse was a leather-dresser, and had his place of business in Cambridgeport. By his own exertions he accumulated a large fortune. He was of a literary turn of mind, and formed during his lifetime a most valuable library of standard and rare works, which, a short time before his death, he presented to the Massachusetts Historical Society. This collection is now known by the donor's name. He left by will a large sum of money to be distributed by his executors for such charitable or literary purposes as they might deem expedient. Of this sum ten thousand dollars were presented to the city of Cambridge, the income of which is to support a course of public lectures in the City Hall. Mr. Dowse was born Dec. 28, 1772, and died Nov. 4, 1856.

Marble monuments on the Dorr and Harris lots, at the right, will be noticed, and next beyond them, on the same side, a most beautifully-sculptured marble on the lot of Levi Brigham. At the left, on the corner of Spruce Avenue, is a monument on the Dillaway lot. This monument always at-

THE STORY STATUE.
See page 40.

tracts attention; it is exceedingly appropriate in design, and is most beautifully executed. On the left is the marble monument on the Adams lot, recently erected by Alvin Adams. It is of pure white marble, exceedingly rich in design and beautiful in execution. On the corner of Pine and Yarrow Paths is the Homer lot, with a large freestone monument, in form like a sarcophagus, —

In memory of George Joy Homer, a citizen of Boston, who was born Jan. 4, 1782, and died June 7, 1843, — an intelligent and upright merchant, a friend and benefactor of the poor, a guide and consoler of the erring, tender and true in all the relations of domestic life, a devout and sincere Christian, — this monument is erected, to commemorate his virtues, by many friends.

On the right, opposite the Homer lot, is a very neat and appropriate monument, erected to the memory of Sumner Hudson.

Turn to the left, passing around the Homer lot, into Yarrow Path.

YARROW PATH.

A small marble monument on the right is to the memory of Thomas Green Fessenden, well known to a former generation as a writer on agricultural and kindred subjects, and for many years editor of the New England Farmer. He died Nov. 11, 1837. This monument was erected by the Massachusetts Society for Promoting Agriculture. There is a small marble column on the Buck lot at the left. Marble monuments on the Winsor and Turner lots, at the left, are noticeable. Each of these monuments is in the form of a sarcophagus. In the rear of these lots may be seen a lot with a very singular granite inclosure, the property of Messrs. Chaplin and Dexter, designed by the latter. On the Robinson lot at the left there is a small figure of a kneeling child, and another of a sleeping infant. On the right is a marble monument to the memory of Edward Dillingham Bangs, for many years Secretary of the Commonwealth; and in the same inclosure is another to the memory of George P. Bangs, a well-known Boston merchant. On the Whipple lot at the right is a marble bearing this inscription : —

We have eternity for Love's communion.

The Whitney lot, on the left, is very appropriately arranged. The sculpture of Little Emily in the Binney lot, at the right, generally attracts considerable attention. It is a fine specimen of art.

MONUMENT ON THE LOT OF ALVIN ADAMS.

See page 44.

> Shed not for her the bitter tear,
>> Nor give the heart to vain regret ;
> 'Tis but the casket that lies here,
>> The gem that filled it sparkles yet.

The Dana monument, of granite, may be seen at the right, and also the Kendrick monument, of marble, surmounted by a cross.

Turn to the right, and pass into Fir Avenue.

While standing in Fir Avenue, the Magoun monument, one of the most beautiful in the grounds, will be noticed at the left ; a large pedestal of marble, with two weeping female figures, one bending over the other, sculptured above it.

> A household's tomb, to Faith how dear !
> A part have gone ; part linger here ;
> United all in love and hope,
>> One household still !

> Together we shall sleep,
> Together may we rise,
> And sing our morning hymn,
>> One household still !

Leave the Magoun monument on the left, pass on through Fir Avenue, and turn to the left into Elm Avenue.

ELM AVENUE.

On the left is a small marble monument on the Sargent lot. At a short distance to the right will be seen the Norcross lot, upon which is a beautiful marble column and pedestal, surmounted by an urn, to the memory of

Otis Norcross, died Nov. 22, 1847, aged 42. He loved his fellow-men. Never mortal left this lower earth better prepared to pass death's scrutiny. Samuel D. Norcross died Dec. 21, 1839, aged 21. An affectionate son and brother, and true friend. Sleep ! thou who wast weary with the march of life ! Sleep on !

Return to Elm Avenue, and view the Stedman monument on the right, and the Knight monument on the same side of the avenue.

Wm. H. Knight, born in England. Elizabeth S. Knight, born in Framingham, May 22, 1794 ; died in Boston, Sept. 10, 1852, in the hope of eternal life. " One Lord, one Faith, one Baptism." " God is love." " Thy loving kindness is better than life." " In Thy presence is fulness of joy." " At Thy right hand are pleasures forevermore."

On the left are the marble monuments on the lots of J. Stedman, Solomon Piper, and Henry A. Reed. That on the latter is inscribed, —

> Henry A. Reed, died May 20, 1852.

> No more to suffer, but for aye to be
> In God's eternal sunshine, blest and free.

MAGOUN MONUMENT.

See page 46.

Turn to the left into Mistletoe Path ; after passing through which, turn to the left into Greenbrier Path, the first path on the left.   Pass through Greenbrier Path, and turn to the right into Fir Avenue.

FIR AVENUE.

The visitor will now pass the Boynton lot on the right, the Jones lot on the left, the Magoun monument again, on the right, and reach the Shaw lot on the same side.   There is in this lot a granite obelisk with base, at the top of which is sculptured a hand pointing upwards.

Boast not thyself of to-morrow.
This is the state of man: to-day he puts forth the tender leaves of hope, to-morrow blossoms ; the third day comes a frost, a killing frost, and (—) nips his root.

A beautiful marble column in the Chamberlin lot at the right will be noticed as very appropriate.   There is also a small marble monument in the Harris lot at the left.

Turn into Heliotrope Path on the left, examine the Gardner monument, and then return to Fir Avenue.

The Gardner lot contains Mr. Dexter's sculpture of Little Frank, in marble, beneath a freestone temple.   On returning to Fir Avenue, the Reed lot will be passed at the right, and on the left will be seen a slab of marble, erected to the memory of Lucius Bolles, D. D., with the Bible, belt, and crown.

Girt about with truth.   Born at Ashford, Conn., Sept. 25, 1779 ; died at Boston, Mass., Jan. 5, 1844.

On the left is a small white marble obelisk in the Ordway lot.   Mr. Ordway is a musician, and the harp on the front of the obelisk, together with the inscription below, are very appropriate.   There is this inscription : —

Staccato is life — Presto is death — Placido the grave.

Turn to the left into Columbine Path, examine the Thayer and Binney monuments, pass between the two into Heath Path, and then return to Fir Avenue.

The Binney monument is one of the finest in the Cemetery.   On the back is a large weeping female figure, and on the front a beautiful figure of an angel.   It is inscribed, —

Amos Binney, M. D., died at Rome, February 18, 1847, aged 41.

Returning to Fir Avenue, we pass on the right the Poor, Pratt, Leland, and Dunbar lots, all appropriate ; that of John H. Kelsey on the left.   The weeping figure in this lot is beautifully executed.   On the right is Dr. S. O. Richardson's monument to the memory of Ella, a white marble

BINNEY MONUMENT.

See page 18.

temple, with a sleeping child therein. On the right is the public lot called St. John's. There is nothing particularly worthy of the visitor's notice here, except a tablet to the memory of Capt. Josiah Cleveland, a soldier of the revolution.

To the memory of Captain Josiah Cleveland, of Owego, N, Y., this tablet is erected by those among whom he departed this life, and who felt respect for his private virtues and gratitude for his public services. He was born at Canterbury, Conn., Dec. 3, 1753. He died at Charlestown, Mass., June 30, 1843. He was an officer of the Army of Freedom. He served his country bravely and faithfully through the whole war of the Revolution. He fought her battles at Bunker Hill, Harlem Heights, White Plains, Trenton, Princeton, Monmouth, and Yorktown. He sustained an unblemished reputation, and lived in the practice of every Christian virtue. He loved, feared, and served God. In the ninetieth year of his age he journeyed nearly five hundred miles from his home to be present at the celebration of the completion of the monument on Bunker Hill. He lived to witness that memorable spectacle. He was satisfied. He laid down quietly, and yielded up his breath near the scene of his first conflict with the enemies of his country. He came among strangers; he died among friends.

The Ritchie monument on the right, and the Comer monument on the left, will then be passed.

Turn to the left into Spruce Avenue.

SPRUCE AVENUE.

On this avenue the first lots that attract attention are those of French and Pearl, on the right; the next, that of Robert C. Mackay, on the same side. The latter contains a very appropriate marble monument, with the Bible and cross sculptured upon it, and these lines : —

I am the Resurrection and the Life. He that believeth in me, though he were dead, yet shall he live.
Then shall the dust return to the earth as it was, and the spirit shall return unto God who gave it.

Several other monuments on this avenue are worthy of particular mention, but our limited space forbids our referring to them at length. It will be sufficient for our purpose, to call the visitor's attention to them, to say that we refer to the Wesson monument on the left, the Fitz, on the left, the Tubbs, on the right, G. C. Richardson, on the left, and the Blanchard monument on the right. The Austin lot on the left has a slab with this inscription : —

Joseph Austin, of Boston, Mass., died July 27, 1847, aged 85.

His soul to Him who gave it rose ;
God led it to its long repose,
Its glorious rest !
And though the good man's sun has set,
Its light shall linger round us yet,
Bright, radiant, blest !

RICHARDSON MONUMENT.

See page 50.

The monument on the Wells lot at the right is a peculiar but very appropriate one. The material is of a grayish sandstone. There is no ornament whatever about it ; but near its top it is cut through from side to side, showing a hollow cross on each of its four sides. On the Watson lot at the right there is a large marble Gothic monument, and a small marble column on the Heath lot on the same side of the avenue. The Stickney and Wason monuments on the right also deserve attention. At the corner of Heliotrope Path the visitor will have an opportunity to view the monument on the Allen lot. This monument has been frequently noticed by many as being one of the most appropriate and beautifully-executed in the Cemetery. It is to the memory of

Samuel P. Allen, died Jan. 24, 1850, aged 36 years.

This monument is highly ornamental, and is of a design exceedingly difficult to describe in the limited space at command. It should be noticed by all visitors. From this spot may be seen, at the right, the fronts of the Franklin and Dowse monuments.

After having viewed these, the visitor will return, and turn to the left into Eglantine Path.

EGLANTINE PATH.

The first monument in this path is one on the left, —

In memory of Benjamin Thompson, of Charlestown, Mass. Born Aug. 5, 1798. Died Sept. 24, 1852. He possessed the entire confidence and respect of his fellow-citizens, was honored with many places of official trust, and, at the time of his death, was a Representative in the Congress of the United States. His amenity and integrity, mature judgment and devotion to duty, gave dignity to his public station. His strength of love for home and kindred made him the idol of his family. The sincerity of his friendship, the purity of his conversation, and the charm of his companionship endeared him to all, and made his private life the scene of his chief enjoyment and of the most delightful manifestations of his character. Sacred to the memory of his life and virtues.

There is an uncommonly neat and appropriate monument on the Tilton lot at the left, to the memory of

Stephen Tilton, died Jan. 12, 1857, aged 66 years.

There is a beautiful marble monument on the Dana lot, at the right, and there is also on the Reed lot another of marble, with a wreath and cross at the top.

Therefore be ye also ready ; for in such an hour as ye think not the Son of Man cometh.

William Gordon Reed, died in Paris Feb. 13, 1849, aged 37 years. His remains were here interred the 6th of the following April.

PERKINS MEMORIAL.

See page 56.

On the Eldridge lot there is a very large granite monument, with a slab inserted in the front, with a bass relief in white marble, of Christ blessing little children.

Turn to the left, pass between the Pierce lot, No. 991, and the Bayley lot, 1539, and turn to the right into Cypress Avenue.

CYPRESS AVENUE.

On the right there is a marble slab to the memory of Dr. W. G. Chandler and two children, erected by his wife.

Rest with your father, beloved children, till the morn of the Resurrection dawns.

The Blake, Baxter, and Norcross monuments on the left will be passed before reaching the St. James public lot on the right.   On the Norcross lot is a large and beautiful marble monument to the memory of

Father, Mother, Son.

There is also in this lot a smaller pedestal, upon which is the image of a sleeping child, inscribed, "Little Addison," and over the grave of the child is inscribed upon the headstone, —

I have laid him under this fresh green sod,
With a heart almost broken, yet trusting in God ;
The heart and the form which I cherished here,
I shall meet again in a happier sphere.

The various memorials in the public lot are worthy of examination, but our limited space will prevent our referring to them.

Nearly opposite the public lot is a small path, through which pass, and turn into Hibiscus Path, the second path on the left, examining the Thayer monument on the right side of the short path.

HIBISCUS PATH.

On the right, on the lot of the late Rev. Frederick T. Gray, will be seen an exceedingly appropriate memorial. It represents an open Bible upon a pulpit desk, and carved upon the book is, —

Whosoever liveth and believeth in me shall never die.   Believest thou this?

On the Garrett lot, at the right, is a marble obelisk ; on the Adams lot, at the left, a tall marble column, with urn and drapery.   We next reach the lot on which has been erected a freestone slab, with cross above, —

To the memory of John Farrar, Professor of Mathematics and Natural Philosophy of Harvard College ; a lucid, eloquent, and devout expositor of the material laws of the universe ; in his manners, dignified, simple, refined ; in his dealings with others, kind and upright.   After

WARD MEMORIAL.

See page 56.

fourteen years of painful disease, borne with patience and serenity, he died as he had lived, an humble disciple of Jesus Christ.

After passing the Thacher monument on the right, the visitor will turn to the right, and pass into Cypress Avenue.

CYPRESS AVENUE.

As the visitor turns into this avenue he will see on his right the beautiful monument erected on the Humphrey lot, representing Hope with an anchor ; and on the left a small but neat and appropriate memorial to the late Leopold Herwig. On the right again will be seen a broken granite column, marked Lienow ; then the Gould monument on the left. The ornamental lot of Messrs. Tisdale and Hewins will be noticed on the left, and will undoubtedly attract the particular attention of the visitor. To the great credit of the owners of this lot, it may be remarked, that it is always in the best order, and the keeping it so seems to be to them a pleasure. We wish we could make the same remark concerning all the lots in the Cemetery. There are a few that seem to be totally neglected. On the right the Bridge lot will be passed.

Turn to the right, and pass into Central Avenue.

CENTRAL AVENUE.

On the left, the dog on the Perkins lot will first be noticed. This is a most beautifully-sculptured representation of a Newfoundland dog, the owner of which was buried beneath the monument. The dog died soon after its owner.

In the rear of the Perkins lot may be seen a memorial to the memory of

Nathaniel Goddard, born June, 1767. Died Aug. 9, 1853. A good man and a just.

On the left is the Billings monument ; on the right, the Ward — a marble slab, with a full length female figure, in relief ; on the left, the Alden ; on the right, a small circular marble column on the Lothrop lot ; and on the left, the Kittredge monument. On the right is a memorial to the memory of John Parker.

The memory of the just is blessed. Their works do follow them.

On the same lot are also memorials inscribed, —

Mrs. Dorcas Sargent Chandler. Blessed are the pure in heart, for they shall see God.
Epes Sargent, Jr. Living and dying, we are the Lord's.
Catherine Sargent.
> Think not her hopes of heaven were vainly based
> On the rare virtues that her long life graced.
> She built not on the sand, but on a Stone,
> And rose sublime, sustained by Christ alone.

ALLEN MONUMENT.

See page 52

Dorcas Sargent. She took upon her the yoke of Christ. She learned of Him, and she found rest unto her soul.

Epes Sargent. He walked in the light of his Saviour's countenance, and in his righteousness was he exalted.

On the monument in the Trull lot, on the right, is inscribed, —

Thus passes away the glory of the world.

The next lot on the right is owned by John M. and David Barnard. It incloses a marble monument, on which are inscribed the names of infant children, and these words : —

This place, the place of our sepulture, is wholly to be disregarded by us, but not to be neglected by our surviving friends.

The Abbe lot on the left will next be passed, on which is an appropriately-designed marble monument, with a hand pointing upward sculptured upon its front, and this inscription : —

There is rest in Heaven.

Christ is the resurrection and the life; he that believeth in Him, though he were dead, yet shall he live. Although worms destroy our bodies, yet in our flesh shall we see God, whom we shall see for ourselves and our eyes shall behold. In these sentiments we repose.

Jesus, to thy most faithful hand
  Our living souls we trust ;
Our flesh shall wait for thy command,
  While crumbling into dust.

O thou majestic Saviour, come,
  That jubilee proclaim,
And teach us language fit to praise
  So great, so dear a name.

In the same lot there is a monument marked B. Burgess, with a bird sculptured on its front, bearing upwards in its beak a scroll, and upon it the words : —

This is not our home.
God will redeem our souls from the power of the grave.
Where, O Death, is now thy sting, O Grave thy victory, where?

Also, in the same lot, a marble monument marked Gibbs.

When Christ, who is our life, shall appear, then shall ye also appear with Him in glory.

On the Phelps lot, on the left, there is a freestone Gothic monument ; and marble ones on the Barney and Frost lots, on the right. Beyond these, on the left, there is a broken marble column, to the memory of

Wm. W. Peck, died Sept. 12, 1846, aged 36 years. The Lord knoweth the days of the upright, and their inheritance shall be forever.

On the Milton lot, at the left, is a small, peculiar monument of marble, —

In memory of departed relatives.
Remembrance strews their graves with flowers.

BALLOU MONUMENT.
See page 60.

On the right there is a marble obelisk on the Brown lot. On the same side, on Ailanthus Path, will be noticed the granite tombs of Samuel O. Mead and William Read.

On the left is the statue of Rev. Hosea Ballou. The commemorative statue of this eminent man, who was so universally beloved and respected for his talents, his life devoted to the promulgation of the word of God, to the building up and extension of the church to which he belonged, and to the practice of all the virtues which adorn, beautify, and dignify social existence, was purchased by subscriptions from the Universalist denomination at large, and was executed by Edward A. Brackett, the well-known sculptor.

Those who from long familiarity with the departed are entitled to express an opinion of the artist's fidelity, are satisfied with the result of his labors, while viewed simply as a work of art, we think that a high rank will be accorded to this effort. The statue is of pure white marble, standing upon a granite pedestal. There is no inscription, recording in florid terms the titles of the deceased to love and veneration ; none such were needed. His memory requires no monument : his epitaph is written in the hearts of those who loved him ; his fame will live with that great body of Christians, which he saw increase from a small band of worshippers to a widespread, powerful, and influential denomination, and with whose progress and development he was identified through a long, laborious, self-sacrificing life. His reputation will live outside even of the wide circle of his followers, among all who cherish the memory of the good, the pure, the wise, the charitable, and the sacrificing.

The Rev. Mr. Ballou was born April 30, 1771, in Richmond, N. H., and died in Boston, on the 7th of June, 1852 ; a long life vouchsafed to but few among the sons of men. Yet to the last his mind was active, and to within a few weeks of his death, he was constantly occupied in the sacred duties of his calling.

> " We weave no dirge for thee, —
>   It should not call a tear
> To know that thou art free ;
>   Thy home. — it was not here !
> Joy to thee. man of God ;
>   Thy heaven-course is begun ;
> Unshrinking thou hast trod
>   Death's vale, — thy race is done! "

STETSON MONUMENT.

6

See page 62.

Turn to the left, pass between the Gray and Prince tombs and the Stetson monument, and turn to the right into Geranium Path.

GERANIUM PATH.

Notice the beautiful Stetson monument on the right, one of the most noted in the Cemetery. As a memorial to the dead, it is appropriate in design and execution, and viewed as a work of art alone it always attracts the notice of the visitor. It bears the following inscription : —

The memory of the Just is blessed.
The dead in Christ repose in guarded rest. Hope, in their graves, hath her never-dying lamp, and throws upon their treasured dust a steady ray, full of immortality.

The memorials on the Upton and Swallow lots, at the left, will next attract attention. The Walker monument, on the right, has this inscription : —

My flesh shall slumber in the ground
Till the last trumpet's joyful sound ;
Then burst the bands with sweet surprise,
And in my Saviour's image rise.

On the same lot there is a memorial to James C. Peverley.

Sleep, loved one ; thy sufferings all are o'er ;
Pain ne'er again can heave thy breast,
Nor anguish wake thy spirit more
From its eternal, quiet rest.

On the same lot there is a small marble memorial, marked with this touching inscription : —

My Wife. Mrs. S. P. W. Crocker, died May 18, 1856, aged 47 years and 10 months. She was always so pleasant.

We next pass the Harrington, Rice, Greene, Gates, and Labree lots, on all of which there are appropriate memorials.

Turn to the right into Beech Avenue, and pass through Beech Avenue toward Central Square.

CENTRAL SQUARE.

On the left will be seen a memorial to Martha Whiting, —

In memory of our Teacher, who died Aug. 22, 1853, aged 58 years. She hath done what she could. Erected by the pupils of the Charlestown Female Seminary.

On the right, between Beech and Central Avenues, may be seen the monument, probably the first erected within the grounds, to the memory of Hannah Adams, and inscribed, —

To Hannah Adams, Historian of the Jews and Reviewer of the Christian Sects, this monument is erected by her female friends First Tenant of Mount Auburn. She died Dec. 15, 1831, aged 76.

WHITING MEMORIAL.

See page 62

The lot on which this monument stands is a very small one, and the monument itself is simple and unpretending. It will be noticed that the inscription declares that the inscription declares that Miss Adams was the " first tenant of Mount Auburn." This is not the *exact* truth. The records of the Corporation show that the *first* burial in Mount Auburn was of a child of James Boyd, July 6, 1832, in lot No. 182, on Mountain Avenue. The second burial was of Mrs. Hastings, wife of Thomas Hastings, of East Cambridge, July 12, 1832, in lot 301, on the same avenue. Mrs. Hastings was therefore, although she died many years previously, the first adult buried in Mount Auburn, as the monument on the Hastings lot declares. There was doubtless no misstatement intended, in relation to Miss Adams, by the writer of the inscription. She died in December, 1831, only about three months after the Cemetery was consecrated. It was impossible to place her body in Mount Auburn at that season of the year; and it was in all probability placed in some temporary place of deposit in Boston, with the intention of removing it as soon as the weather would permit. It may have been that the placing the body in a receiving tomb in Boston was considered the same as a burial at Mount Auburn to all intents and purposes ; or it may have been that the monument was prepared in anticipation of the removal of the body to Mount Auburn, but that some delay occurred, and it was not deemed necessary to be at the expense of altering the inscription. However this may be, Miss Adams was not the " first tenant of Mount Auburn," but the ninth, her remains having been placed in the Cemetery November 12, 1832.

Pass around the Square, to the left, and between the Knight lot, No. 662, on right, and the Smith lot, No. 48, on left, pass in front of the Murray monument, No. 587.

John Murray, Preacher of the Gospel. Born in Alton, Eng., Dec. 10, 1741 ; died in Boston Sept. 3, 1815. Re-interred beneath this stone June 8, 1837.

Pass through the narrow path at the right, passing near the Dana lot, and then turn to the left, into Walnut Avenue.

WALNUT AVENUE.

On this avenue are various tombs, appropriate in every respect, but not sufficiently attractive to the visitor to need particular mention. The lot of the Scots' Charitable Asso-

MONUMENT TO THE MEMORY OF HANNAH ADAMS.

See pages 62 and 64.

ciation, on the right, is noticeable from the peculiarity of its railing. The Wales, Salisbury, and Welles monuments, on the right, will next be noticed, particularly the latter to the memory of John Welles; then, on the left, the Smith and Tilson lots; the Sumner, Hall, and Kimball on the right. A short distance to the right will be seen the monument erected to the memory of the various members of the Osgood family, of which Mrs. Frances Sargent Osgood, the poetess, was one. A harp with broken strings surmounts this monument. The Holmes monument, on the left, will then be noticed, and on the same side that to the memory of

Noah Worcester. Born at Hollis, N. H., Nov. 25, 1758. Died at Brighton, Mass., Oct. 31, 1837, aged 79 years. Blessed are the peacemakers, for they shall be called the Children of God.

The Field monument on the right, a marble obelisk, deserves the attention of the visitor.

Turn to the right, and pass around the Field lot into Pyrola Path.

PYROLA PATH.

There are several beautiful memorials on this path, but the most of which we cannot, for want of space, mention in particular, beyond giving the names. On the left there is one to the memory of Barnabas Bates, "Father of Cheap Postage" — a tall marble obelisk on a massive pedestal; one of granite on the Tyler lot at right; one on a lot owned by Charles Leighton and Benjamin Beal; the peculiar whiteness of the granite used for this monument is worthy of more than a passing notice; the Edwards lot on right, with a peculiarly-constructed railing, in which the hourglass is plainly observable; and the beautiful marble monument erected to the memory of the Rev. Addison Searle, a Chaplain in the Navy, buried at sea, Aug. 2, 1850. We now reach the Fuller lot, on the left, in which there are tributes to the memory of the late Hon. Timothy Fuller, who died Oct. 1, 1835, his daughter Mrs. Margaret Fuller Ossoli, and various other members of the family. We give the inscription on the Ossoli tablet in full. Above the tablet is a cross, beneath which is sculptured a portrait of Mrs. Ossoli, with book and sword.

In memory of Margaret Fuller Ossoli. Born in Cambridge, Mass., May 23, 1810. By birth a child of New England — by adoption a citizen of Rome — by genius belonging to the world. In youth an insatiate student, seeking the highest culture; in riper years, teacher, writer, critic of literature and art; in maturer age, companion and helper of many earnest reformers in America and Europe. And of her husband,

OSSOLI MEMORIAL.

See page 66.

Giovanni Angelo, Marquis Ossoli. He gave up rank, station, and home for the Roman Republic, and for his wife and child. And of the child, Angelo Eugene Philip Ossoli, born in Rieti, Italy, Sept. 5, 1848, whose dust reposes at the foot of this stone.

They passed from this life together by shipwreck July 19, 1850. United in life by mutual love, labors, and trials, the merciful Father took them together, and in death they were not divided.

The rough freestone cross on the Eliot lot will be passed, after noticing which the visitor will *continue on, turn to the left, passing around the Dehon lot, into Bellwort Path, and then cross over again in the same way into Trefoil Path, the next path beyond, and turn to the left.*

TREFOIL PATH.

There is nothing noticeable on this path but a large inclosure of four lots, with a large granite obelisk in the centre, on each side of which is one of the names of Otis, Bates, Rice, and Bordman.

Pass through Trefoil Path a short distance only, and turn into Tulip Path, the first path on the right.

TULIP PATH.

The Gahne monument will be noticed here; also the Brooks lot, on the left; the Payson, on the right; and the Devens, Hubbard, and Robbins lots on the right.

Turn to the right into Walnut Avenue; pass through Walnut Avenue, noticing the Crockett and Snow lots on the left, and then turn to the left into Mountain Avenue.

MOUNTAIN AVENUE.

There are several tombs on this avenue. On the left, as you turn to the tower, is the Hastings lot before referred to. It is really three lots with one inclosure. On each lot is a large marble monument, with an urn above. The centre one, the Hastings monument, has this inscription : —

Mary Robbins, wife of Thomas Hastings, died July 12, 1818, aged 26. The first adult buried at Mount Auburn.

The Bemis monument is at the left of the Hastings memorial, and the Kimball monument on the right, the latter inscribed, —

Ebenezer Kimball, died Aug. 14, 1839, aged 47 years. A kind husband, a beloved father, and a good citizen. He possessed, in an unwonted degree, those qualities of head and heart which endeared him to those among whom he dwelt.

The visitor can now ascend to the top of the Tower, from which he will be enabled to obtain, as has been before remarked, one of the finest prospects to be had in the suburbs of Boston. The city, the country towns around, Charles

THE TOWER.

See pages 25 and 66.

River at the foot, all contribute to make up a view that, for real beauty of natural scenery, few will have an opportunity to see surpassed.

After having descended, the visitor will pass around the Tower, and enter Hazel Path.

Just before entering Hazel Path, there will be seen, on the left, two large granite obelisks, the largest in the Cemetery, erected to the memory of various members of the Fuller family. On the right will be seen a small obelisk on the Eaton lot.

HAZEL PATH AND HARVARD HILL.

Pass through Hazel Path, passing the Farnum tomb, on the left; then turn to the right and pass across Harvard Hill; pass the Kirkland and Ashmun monuments.

On Harvard Hill, the visitor will notice the monument to the memory of Rev. John Thornton Kirkland, formerly President of Harvard College, with an inscription, in Latin. Near this memorial is another, inscribed as follows : —

Here lies the body of John Hooker Ashmun, Royall Professor of Law in Harvard University, who was born July 3, 1800, and died April 1st, 1833. In him the science of law appeared native and intuitive. He went behind precedents to principles, and books were his helpers, never his masters. There was the beauty of accuracy in his understanding, and the beauty of uprightness in his character. Through the slow progress of the disease which consumed his life, he kept unimpaired his kindness of temper and superiority of intellect. He did more work sick than others in health. He was fit to teach at an age when common men are beginning to learn, and his few years bore the fruit of long life. A lover of truth, an obeyer of duty, a sincere friend, and a wise instructor. His pupils raise this stone to his memory.

In the vicinity of the Kirkland and Ashmun monuments may be seen those of others connected with the College. This spot is one of the most romantic in the Cemetery. It is visited by but a very few compared with the whole number who enter the grounds. The stranger, therefore, who may never have an opportunity to visit Mount Auburn a second time, should by no means omit to stop here for a few moments.

After viewing the Ashmun memorial, keep to the left, and descend the hill; pass in front of the Fuller tomb, on Woodbine Path; then ascend Cedar Hill, alongside of the Appleton monumental temple.

CEDAR HILL.

On Cedar Hill will be seen the very beautiful marble temple, beneath which rest the remains of the Hon. Samuel Appleton. A cut of this structure will give the reader a better idea of it than words.

APPLETON MONUMENT.

See page 70.

From this spot Consecration Dell may be seen, at the left.
Presuming the visitor to be standing with the Appleton monument at his right, he should then continue on nearly in a straight line, slightly inclining to the right, however, descend the hill, and enter Lily Path.

LILY PATH.

The Richards lot, on the left, and the Gray lot, on the right, are the only ones noticeable in this path.   On the former there is a beautiful granite memorial, and on the latter a large marble column, surmounted by an urn.

The visitor will then turn to the right, into Hemlock Path, the first path on the right, noticing, as he turns, the sun dial on the corner lot at the left.

HEMLOCK PATH.

On the right will be seen three large lots inclosed in one, each of which has upon it a marble monument, one marked Young, one Farnsworth, and one Loring.   The first-named is also inscribed : —

In memory of Rev. Alexander Young, D.D., born in Boston, Sept. 22, 1800.   Graduated at Harvard College 1820.   Ordained Pastor of the New South Church in Boston, Jan. 19, 1825.   Died March 16, 1854, in the 29th year of his ministry.   An accomplished scholar, a profound theologian, a consistent and faithful minister, his character was marked with piety, truth, honor, and a tender sense of domestic ties.   In the midst of his usefulness, surrounded with affectionate relatives and friends, he was unexpectedly summoned away, and found ready.   This token of respect and love has been erected by his bereaved congregation.

On the right will be noticed the Humphrey and Wheeler lot, and the Fairbanks and McDonald lots on the left.

Turn to the left into Willow Avenue, the second path on the left.

WILLOW AVENUE.

On the right is a small marble obelisk, on the Williams lot, inscribed : —

I know that THOU wilt bring me to death and to the house appointed for all living.

On the right, the Waterhouse lot should be particularly noticed, and, on the same side, the Bradlee monument.   On the left, the Randall monument will then be noticed. There is a small marble monument on the Pratt lot, on the left, which bears this inscription : —

> O, when a mother meets on high
> The babes she lost in infancy,
> Hath she not then, for pains and fears,
>   The day of woe, the watchful night,
> For all her sorrows, all her tears,
>   An over payment of delight?

The visitor will then pass the Chamberlain, Prentice, Bartlett and Carr, Cushing and Knapp lots, on the left. In the latter is a marble slab to the memory of

John Knapp, died March 19, 1849, Æt. 70 years. In him were blended the tenderest affections, learning without ostentation, and worth without pretension.

The visitor will have an opportunity to view, from this spot, the beautiful Meadow Pond.

The Torrey lot, and the Thayer lot, on the left, will next be passed. On the latter is a very peculiar three-sided monument, to the memory of Amasa Thayer and wife, and inscribed, —

—— They meet to part no more,
And, with celestial welcome, greet
On an immortal shore.

There are two very appropriate, but similarly constructed, monuments on the Norcross and Hurlburt lots, on the left. The Buckingham lot will next be reached, in which rest the remains of several members of the family of the Hon. Joseph T. Buckingham, of Cambridge, formerly editor of the Boston Courier. A neat marble memorial was erected to the memory of Edwin Buckingham, a son, a young man of more than ordinary promise, born 1810. He edited, until his death, the New England Magazine. He died at sea, and his loss was sincerely regretted.

" Rest, loved one, rest — beneath the billow's swell,
Where tongue ne'er spoke, where sunlight never fell;
Rest — till the God who gave thee to the deep,
Rouse thee, triumphant, from the long, long sleep.

The Howe and Wyman lots, on the right, and the Taylor lot at the left, will then be seen; after noticing which, the visitor will *turn to the left into Narcissus Path*.

NARCISSUS PATH.

The path to be followed winds along by the left side of Forest Pond, both sides of which are principally devoted to tombs. The Hosmer lot, on the right; the monuments on the Wingate and Webster lots, at the left; the Pierce, Carnes, Winchester, Samuel Henshaw, and Cushing tombs, will be particularly noticed. On the Ayer lot there is a memorial to Lucy Adelaide Ayer, died Aug. 10, 1845, aged 21.

Sleep on, sweet one, thy rest has come;
'T is for myself I mourn,
And for this precious babe, to whom
Thou never must return.

7

Lone are my paths and sad the hours
Now thy meek smile is gone;
But O ! a brighter home than ours
In heaven is now thine own.
Blessed are the pure in heart.

On the left will be noticed the lot in which rest the remains of the late eminent jurist, Joseph Story, first President of the Proprietors of Mount Auburn.

Keep to the right, and turn into Alder Path; pass through Alder Path, and turn to the right into Locust Avenue, and turn again to the right into Beech Avenue.

BEECH AVENUE.

There is on this avenue a small granite memorial to Mrs. Sarah T. Holt, inscribed, —

Farewell ! departed and beloved spirit ;
Our heavy loss is thy eternal gain.

Passing along to the left, will be seen very appropriate, and in some instances beautiful monuments, on the Emery, Boardman, S. F. Coolidge, Green, Jacob Bigelow, and Gould lots; and also on the Harrod, Nichols, Fales, Greenwood, Tirrell, Coburn, and Ellis lots, at the right.

Turn to the right into Linden Path.

LINDEN PATH.

On the Fisher lot there is a monument to the memory of several infant children, inscribed, —

The mother gave, in tears and pain,
The flowers she most did love ;
She knew she should find them all again
In the fields of light above.

The Bird lot, on the right, and the Barnard lot, on the left, will then be passed. On the right a monument has been erected to the memory of

Samuel B. Doane, obit. Sept. 3, 1845, aged 63 years. He is not here, but has ascended to the bosom of his Father and his God.

The Thaxter lot, on the right, and the broken marble column, on the left, will attract attention.

The visitor will then continue on, almost in a straight line, into Catalpa Path.

CATALPA PATH.

On this path there are but few monuments. One on the Davis lot, at the right, and a Gothic freestone erection on the Hatch lot, on the same side, will be particularly noticed.

Continue on, keeping to the left, into Indian Ridge Path.

INDIAN RIDGE PATH.

The beautiful marble monument on the Merrill lot, at the right, will here receive attention ; after noticing which, continue on, and *turn to the right into Central Avenue, which leads directly to the Gate.*

It is not to be supposed that the foregoing route and description embrace *all* the objects worthy of notice in the Cemetery. If the route has been followed, the visitor has seen the *principal* objects of interest within the grounds ; he has visited the most attractive places, and viewed the most interesting monuments, including the larger number of those most frequently inquired for by strangers ; in fact, the visitor has seen sufficient to enable him to obtain a correct idea of the appearance of the entire Cemetery. There are, however, on other avenues and paths much that is worthy of observation ; and a visit to them would well repay the time occupied in doing so.

By leaving Mount Auburn, and turning to the right, and then passing through Coolidge Avenue, the visitor will reach the Cemetery of the City of Cambridge, where will be found much that will prove interesting.

DIRECTORY TO AVENUES AND PATHS.

AVENUES.

Beech	leads from	Central to Poplar.
Cedar	" "	Cypress to Walnut.
Central	" "	the Gate to Walnut.
Chapel	" "	Central to Pine.
Chestnut	" "	Mountain to Poplar.
Cypress	" "	Central to Walnut.
Elm	" "	Pine to Mistletoe P. and back to Pine.
Fir	" "	Elm to junction of Walnut and Cypress.
Garden	" "	the Gate to Maple.
Larch	" "	Poplar to Maple.
Lawn	" "	Pine, near the Gate, to Spruce.
Laurel	" "	Walnut to the same.
Lime	" "	Maple to the same.
Locust	" "	Poplar to Beech
Magnolia	" "	Mountain to Maple.
Maple	" "	Magnolia, by the easterly and northerly sides of Cemetery, to Garden.
Mountain	" "	Chestnut round the Tower.
Oak	" "	Larch to Willow.
Pine	" "	the Gate to Cypress.
Poplar	" "	Central Square to Chestnut.
Spruce	" "	Pine to Fir, thence by westerly side of Cemetery to Walnut.
Walnut	" "	Central Square to Mountain.
Willow	" "	Poplar, north to Narcissus P., thence back to Walnut.

PATHS.

Acacia	leads from	Spruce Av. to Verbena P.
Acanthus	" "	Larch to Magnolia Av.
Acorn	" "	Maple Avenue to Evergreen P.
Ailanthus	lies between	Central, Cypress, and Cedar Avs.
Alder	leads from	Locust to Poplar Av.
Almond	" "	Indian Ridge P. to the same.
Aloe	" "	Indian Ridge P. to Lime Av.

Amaranth encircles the crown of Harvard Hill.
Anemone   leads from Spruce Av. to Orange P.
Arbutus   "   "   Lime Av. to
Arethusa   "   "   Walnut Av. to Trefoil P.
Asclepias   "   "   Spruce to Fir Av.
Asphodel   "   "   Lawn Av. to
Aster   "   "   Vine to Ivy P.
Azalea   "   "   Spruce Av. to same.
Bellwort   "   "   Spruce Av. to Orange P.
Catalpa   "   "   Indian Ridge P. to same.
Columbine   "   "   Spruce to Fir Av.
Cowslip   "   "   Spruce to Walnut Av.
Daisy   "   "   Locust Av. to Alder P.
Dell   "   "   Vine P., on east and west sides of
    Pond to S. side, thence to Ivy P.
Elder   "   "   Walnut to Spruce Av.
Eglantine   "   "   Fir to Spruce Av.
Evergreen   "   "   Lime Av. to same.
Fern   "   "   Mountain to Walnut Av.
Gentian   "   "   Cypress to Pine and Spruce Avs.
Geranium lies between Central and Beech Avs.
Greenbrier leads from Pine Av. to Mistletoe P.
Harebell   "   "   Walnut Av. to Trefoil P.
Hawthorn   "   "   Chestnut Av., by two ways, to Sweet-
    brier P.
Hazel   "   "   Mountain Av. to Rose P.
Heath   "   "   Spruce to Fir Av.
Heliotrope   "   "   Spruce to Fir Av.
Hemlock   "   "   Poplar Av. to Ivy P.
Hibiscus lies between Cypress and Cedar Avs., entrance
    and exit on Cypress.
Honeysuckle leads from Greenbrier P. to St. John's Lot.
Holly   "   "   Poplar Av. to Ivy P.
Hyacinth   "   "   Cypress to Chapel Av.
Indian Ridge "   "   Central to Larch and Maple Avs.
Iris   "   "   Moss to Ivy P.
Ivy   "   "   Central Square to Woodbine P.
Jasmine   "   "   Chestnut Av. to Hawthorn P.
Laburnum   "   "   Spruce Av. near Lawn to
Lilac   "   "   Willow Av. to Indian Ridge P.
Lily   "   "   Poplar Av. to Aster P., thence to
    Woodbine P.
Linden   "   "   Beech Av. to same.
Lupine   "   "   Cypress to Spruce Av.

7*

Mimosa	leads from	Spruce to Fir Av.
Mistletoe	" "	Elm Av. to St. John's Lot, thence to Fir Av.
Moss	" "	Laurel Avenue to Ivy P.
Myrtle	" "	Chestnut Av. to Hazel P.
Narcissus	" "	Willow Av. to Catalpa P., and around Forest Pond back to Willow Av.
Oleander	" "	Myrtle to Rose P.
Olive	" "	Myrtle to Sweetbrier P.
Orange	" "	Walnut Av. to same.
Orchis	" "	Walnut Av. to Tulip P.
Osier	" "	Willow Av. to Indian Ridge P.
Oxalis	" "	Willow Av. to
Peony	" "	Chapel to Cypress Av.
Petunia	" "	Larch to Magnolia Av.
Pilgrim	" "	Walnut Av. to Snowdrop P.
Primrose	" "	Central Av. to
Pyrola	" "	Spruce Av. to Orange P.
Rhodora	" "	Oak to Larch Av.
Rose	encircles	Harvard Hill.
Rosemary	leads from	Jasmine to Hawthorn P.
Saffron	" "	Spruce Av. to St. John's Lot.
Sedge	" "	Fir Avenue to Heath P.
Sorrel	" "	Spruce to Fir Av.
Snowberry	" "	the Gate to Central Av.
Snowdrop	" "	Walnut to Spruce Av.
Spiræa	" "	Fir Av. to Mistletoe P.
Sumach	" "	Moss to Violet P. and Walnut Av.
Sweetbrier	" "	Chestnut Av. to Hawthorn P.
Sylvan	" "	Walnut to Mountain Av.
Thistle	" "	Spruce Av. to Cowslip P.
Trefoil	" "	Spruce to Walnut Av.
Tulip	" "	Walnut Av. to Trefoil P.
Verbena	" "	Spruce to Fir Av.
Vine	" "	Moss to Iris P.
Woodbine	" "	Hawthorn to Ivy P.
Yarrow	" "	Greenbrier, westerly to Fir. Av., thence easterly to Pine Av.